CRIME AS
STRUCTURED
ACTION

Under the General Editorship of

Daniel Curran, Ph.D.
Professor of Sociology
Chief Academic Officer
Saint Joseph's University
Philadelphia, Pennsylvania

CRIME AS STRUCTURED ACTION

Gender, Race, Class, and Crime in the Making

James W. Messerschmidt

SAGE Publications
International Educational and Professional Publisher
Thousand Oaks   London   New Delhi

For information address:

SAGE Publications, Inc.
2455 Teller Road
Thousand Oaks, California 91320
E-mail: order@sagepub.com

SAGE Publications Ltd.
6 Bonhill Street
London EC2A 4PU
United Kingdom

SAGE Publications India Pvt. Ltd.
M-32 Market
Greater Kailash I
New Delhi 110 048 India

Printed in the United States of America

Library of Congress Cataloging-in-Publication Data

Messerschmidt, James W.
    Crime as structured action: gender, race, class and crime in the
making / author, James W. Messerschmidt.
    Includes bibliographical references and index.
    ISBN 0-7619-0717-3 (cloth: acid-free paper). — ISBN 0-7619-0718-1
(pbk.: acid-free paper)
    1. Crime—Sociological aspects. 2. Criminals—Social conditions.
3. Crime—Sociological aspects—United States—Case studies.
4. Criminals—United States—Social conditions—Case studies.
I. Title.
HM210.M47 1997
364—DC20   96-35669

97 98 99 00 01 02 03 10 9 8 7 6 5 4 3 2 1

Acquiring Editor:	C. Terry Hendrix
Editorial Assistant:	Dale Grenfell
Production Editor:	Michèle Lingre
Production Assistant:	Karen Wiley
Typesetter/Designer:	Janelle LeMaster
Cover Designer:	Candice Harman
Print Buyer:	Anna Chin

For Erik, Jan, and Ulla

Contents

Acknowledgments

This book would have never been written if it were not for the work of Anthony Giddens, Bob Connell, Candace West, Sarah Fenstermaker, and Don Zimmerman. The publications of these individuals represent some of the most important contributions to sociology in recent years and I thank all of them for their invaluable theoretical guidance.

A number of people devoted much time and energy to help make this book possible. I am particularly indebted to Bob Connell and Nancy Jurik, who took time away from their own work to read the entire manuscript and contribute important suggestions on each chapter. Many people also commented on specific portions of the book at various stages of its development: Piers Beirne, Dusan Bjelic, Pat Carlen, Carol Cohn, Kim Cook, Dan Curran, Walter DeKeseredy, Frances Heidensohn, Tony Jefferson, Mark Maier, Bob Miller, Barbara Perry, Nicky Hahn Rafter, Dianne Sadoff, and Diane Vaughan. I thank all of these people for sharing ideas, criticisms, and editorial suggestions.

I owe considerable thanks to Dan Curran (Sage series editor) and to C. Terry Hendrix (Sage editor) for their interest and support of this project.

Most of all, thanks to Erik, Jan, and Ulla for their everlasting love, strength, and encouragement.

Parts of this book have appeared elsewhere in a different form. I thank the publishers for permission to reproduce the following:

Prologue

Structured-Action Theory

Criminologists consistently have advanced gender as the strongest predictor of criminal involvement—it is boys and men who dominate in crime. Arrest, self-report, and victimization data all reflect that boys and men perpetrate more conventional crimes and the more serious of these crimes than do girls and women (Beirne & Messerschmidt, 1995). Men also have a virtual monopoly on the commission of syndicated, corporate, and political crime. Consequently, the capacity to explain this gendered character of crime might stand as *the* "litmus test" for the viability of criminology as a discipline (Allen, 1989). When criminology historically has addressed the relationship between gender and crime, however, it has concentrated on (through an androcentric lens) "women and crime," with little or no attention to the impact of gender on boys and men. It is not that criminologists have ignored boys and men in their quest for uncovering the causes of crime. Rather, as I have shown earlier (Messerschmidt, 1993), major research and theoretical works in criminology are alarmingly gender blind. That is, "although men and boys have been seen as the 'normal subjects,' the gendered content of

1

their legitimate and illegitimate behavior has been virtually ignored" (Messerschmidt, 1993, p. 1). Thus, contemporary criminologists concerned with *the* strongest predictor of criminal involvement have turned to feminist theory for guidance.

Feminism challenged the masculinist nature of the academy by illuminating the patterns of gendered power that social theory to that point had all but ignored. In particular, second-wave feminism[1] secured a permanent role for sexual politics in popular culture and moved analysis of sexuality and gendered power to the forefront of much social thought. Moreover, feminist research, both within and without criminology, spotlighted the nature and pervasiveness of violence against women.

One issue that feminist scholars faced in posing gender questions to the academy concerned the repeated omission and misrepresentation of girls and women. The academy had virtually ignored, trivialized, distorted women's lives and social experiences or all of these. Understandably, then, considerable feminist research has questioned and documented women's social and cultural position in society. Specifically within criminology, since the mid-1970s feminist scholars have examined girls' and women's crime, violence against girls and women, social control of girls and women, and women who work in the criminal justice system (Daly & Chesney-Lind, 1988; Martin & Jurik, 1996; Naffine, 1995). The importance of this feminist work is enormous. It has significantly contributed to and lastingly affected the discipline of criminology. Indeed, not only is the significance of gender to understanding crime more broadly acknowledged in the discipline, but it led, logically, to the critical study of masculinities and crime (DeKeseredy & Schwartz, 1993; Messerschmidt, 1993; Newburn & Stanko, 1994). For increasing numbers of criminologists, boys and men are no longer seen as the "normal subjects"; rather, the social construction of masculinities has come under careful criminological scrutiny. Arguably, when one conceptualizes crime in terms of gender, it is essential to think seriously about boys, men, and masculinities to gain insight into understanding the highly gendered ratio of crime in Western industrialized societies.

Feminist theory, then, provides the starting point for meaningful discussion of gender and crime,[2] and the feminist approach adopted here emphasizes both the meaningful actions of individual agents and the structural features of social settings. Several feminist women and profeminist men have been developing just such a feminist perspective, one whose theoretical object is the situational construction of gender, race, and class (Connell, 1987, 1995a; Martin & Jurik, 1996; Messerschmidt, 1993; Thorne, 1993; West & Fenstermaker, 1993, 1995; West & Zimmerman, 1987). *Crime as Structured Action* contributes to this growing body of work by focusing on people in specific social settings, what they do to construct social relations and social structures, and how these social structures constrain and channel behavior in specific ways.

There is a problem that looms large (especially among critical criminologists) concerning the theoretical links among gender, race, class, and crime. Underscoring this concern, I address how gender, race, and class relations arise within the same ongoing practices. To understand crime, we must comprehend how gender, race, and class relations are part of all social existence—rather than viewing each relation as extrinsic to the others. Crime operates subtly through a complex series of gender, race, and class practices; as such, crime usually is more than a single activity. Thus, what follows is a delineation of the way in which structure and action are woven inextricably in the ongoing activity of "doing" gender, race, class, and crime. I begin with a discussion of social action.

Social Action

Historical and social conditions shape the character and definition of sex, race, and class categories. Each category and its meaning are given concrete expression by the specific social relations and historical context in which they are embedded. Moreover, in specific social situations we consistently engage in sex, race, and class attribution—identifying and categorizing people by appropriate sex, race, and class categories while simultaneously categorizing ourselves to others (West & Fenstermaker, 1995).

Nevertheless, as West and Fenstermaker (1995) argue, "doing" gender, race, and class entails considerably more than the "social emblems" of specific categories. Rather, the social construction of gender, race, and class involves a situated social and interactional accomplishment. In other words, gender, race, and class grow out of social practices in specific settings and serve to inform such practices in reciprocal relation. So, although sex, race, and class categories define social identification, *doing* gender, race, and class systematically corroborates that identification through social interaction. In effect, there is a plurality of forms in which gender, race, and class are constructed: We coordinate our activities to "do" gender, race, and class in situational ways.

Crucial to conceptualizing gender, race, and class as situated accomplishment is the notion of "accountability" (West & Zimmerman, 1987). Because individuals realize that their behavior may possibly be held accountable to others, they configure and orchestrate their actions in relation to how they might be interpreted by others in the particular social context in which they occur. In other words, in their daily activities individuals attempt to be identified socially as, for example, "female" or "male," "African American" or "white," "working class" or "middle class." In this way, accountability "allows individuals to conduct their activities in relation to their circumstances" (West & Fenstermaker, 1993, p. 156), suggesting that gender, race, and class vary by social situation and circumstance. Within social interaction, then, we encourage and expect others to attribute particular categories to us. And we facilitate the ongoing task of accountability by demonstrating we are male or female, African American or white, working class or middle class through concocted behaviors that may be interpreted accordingly. Consequently, we do gender, race, and class differently—depending on the social situation and the social circumstances we encounter. The particular meanings of gender, race, and class are defined in social interaction and, therefore, through personal practice. Doing gender, race, and class, then, renders social action accountable in terms of normative conceptions, attitudes, and activities appropriate to one's category in the specific social situation in which one acts (West & Fenstermaker, 1995).

In this view, therefore, gender, race, and class are accomplished systematically, not imposed on people or settled beforehand, and never static or finished products. Rather, people construct gender,

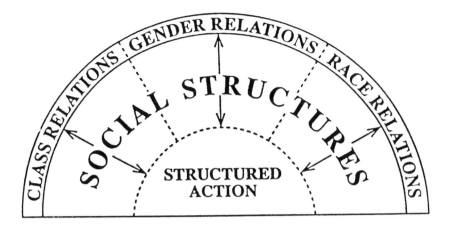

Figure 1.1. Social Relations, Social Structures, and Structured Action
SOURCE: Messerschmidt, 1993:63

race, and class in specific social situations. In other words, people participate in self-regulating conduct whereby they monitor their own and other's social action.

Social Relations, Social Structures, and Structured Action

Although gender, race, and class are "made," so to speak, through the unification of self-regulated practices, these practices do not occur in a vacuum. Instead, they are influenced by the social structural constraints we experience. Social structures, defined here as regular and patterned forms of interaction over time that constrain and channel behavior in specific ways, "only exist as the reproduced conduct of situated actors" (Giddens, 1976, p. 127). As Connell (1987, 1995a) argues, these social structures (e.g., divisions of labor and power and sexuality) are neither external to social actors nor simply and solely constraining; on the contrary, structure is realized only through social action and social action requires structure as its condition (see Figure 1.1). Social structures are enacted by "knowledgeable" human agents (people who know what they are doing and how to do it), and agents act by putting into practice their structured knowledge (Giddens,

1984). Moreover, in certain circumstances, agents improvise or inno-vate in structurally shaped ways that significantly reconfigure the very structures that shaped them (Giddens, 1984). Because people do gender, race, and class in specific social situations, they reproduce and sometimes change social structures. And given that people reproduce gender, race, and class ideals in socially structured specific practices, there are a variety of ways to do them. In other words, specific forms of gender, race, and class are available, encouraged, and permitted, depending on one's position in these social relations. Not only are there numerous ways of constructing masculinity and femininity, we must speak of masculini*ties* and feminini*ties*, there are likewise myr-iad ways of constructing race and class, we must articulate, for example, differing African American identities and middle-class identities. Accordingly, gender, race, and class must be viewed as *structured action*—what people do under specific social structural constraints.

Appropriate, then, is a theory that conceptualizes how gender, race, and class relations arise within the same ongoing structured practices. As with sex, we can identify race and class categories and, therefore, hold people accountable as members of any or all of the categories (West & Fenstermaker, 1995). In other words, the accom-plishment of gender, race, and class occurs simultaneously through social interaction and, as West and Fenstermaker (p. 24) contend, the accountability of persons to these categories is the key to under-standing the maintenance of existing social structures, such as divi-sions of labor and power.

As indicated earlier, divisions of labor and power are social structures that exist in each of the three social relations (Messerschmidt, 1993); and the division of labor in Western indus-trialized societies consists not only of class divisions of labor but also of race and gender. The division of labor refers both to the definition of work (legitimate and illegitimate, paid and unpaid) and how work is allocated. Divisions of labor involve the range of tasks performed in a given position, the nature, meaning, and value of those tasks, and the relations of cooperation, conflict, and authority among positions (Young, 1990, p. 23). As individuals engage in such tasks they produce the three divisions of labor. Consequently, rather than viewing gender, race, and class as discrete "things" that somehow relate to each other, it is important to visualize them as mutually constituting one another (Morgen, 1990, p. 286). That is, throughout daily interaction, social actors simultaneously produce these divisions, as they "do" gender, race, and class.

Moreover, relations of power are embedded in, and reinforced by, divisions of labor. That is, social practices of who does what for whom and the way the results of that labor are appropriated and by whom, operate to construct relations of power and inequality (Young, 1990, p. 50). As such, power is an important structural feature of gender, race, and class relations. Overall, in Western industrialized societies, specific social groups possess, or are restricted from access to, material resources, a situation that places them in an unequal social relation to other groups. Material resources, for example, help construct social structural relations of power, by gender, race, and class, and arrange individuals in relation to other individuals. For example, a manifestation of the gender and race relations of power is the obvious structural fact that white men control the economic, religious, political, and military institutions of authority and coercion in society. A structural process is fashioned whereby "those with power can organize those who are less powerful according to their own ends" (Segal, 1990, p. 261). This occurs at not only large-scale institutional levels but within smaller groups and face-to-face interaction. For example, Connell (1987, p. 107) provides three examples of such face-to-face power in gender relations: "Mr. Barrett the Victorian patriarch forbids his daughter to marry; a bank manager refuses a loan to an unmarried woman; a group of youths rape a girl of their acquaintance." These examples show that power is not solely based on access to material resources and only occurs at the institutional level. Although material resources may clearly enhance gender, race, and class power, they are often unnecessary at the interpersonal level for the actual realization of that power.

Social actors perpetuate and transform these divisions of labor and power within the same interaction; simultaneously, these structures constrain and enable gender, race, and class social action. The result is the ongoing social construction of gender, race, and class relations (see Figure 1.1). Consequently, "doing race" and "doing class" are similar to "doing gender": They render social action accountable in terms of normative conceptions, attitudes, and activities appropriate to one's race and class category in the specific social situation in which one acts (West & Fenstermaker, 1995).[3]

The Salience of Gender, Race, and Class

Nevertheless, the salience of each social relation to influencing crime varies by social situation. Although gender, race, and class are ubiquitous, the significance of each relation shifts with a changing context: In one situation gender and race both may be important for actuating crime; in another social setting, class, or gender, or any combination of the three relations may be relevant. In other words, gender, race, and class are not absolutes and not equally significant in every social setting where crime is realized. That is, accountability to gender, race, and class are not always, in all social situations, equally critical to the social construction of crime.

In this way, then, social relations of gender, race, and class variously join us in a common relationship to others—we share structural space. Consequently, common or shared blocks of knowledge and practices evolve through interaction in which particular gender, race, and class ideals and activities differ in significance. Through such interaction, gender, race, and class become institutionalized, permitting, for example, men and women to draw on such existing, but previously formed, ways of thinking and acting to construct particular race-and-class gender identities for specific settings. The particular criteria of gender, race, and class identities are embedded in the social situations and recurrent practices whereby social relations are structured (Giddens, 1989).

Gender, Sexuality, and Difference

As indicated earlier, power is an important structural feature of gender, race, and class relations. But, in addition to this and specifically with regard to gender (because the case studies that follow emphasize masculinities, femininities, and crime), socially organized power relations among men and among women are constructed historically on the bases of race, class, and sexual preference; that is, in specific contexts some men and some women have greater power than other men and other women. In other words, the capacity to exercise power is, for the most part, a reflection of one's position in social relationships. For example, in the antebellum South, "white men as husbands had control over their wives and as fathers control over their children's marriages and access to family property, but black male slaves had no such patriarchal rights" (Ferguson, 1991, p. 113). Moreover, in late 19th- and early 20th-century California and Hawaii, most domestic servants in white, middle-class households were Asian men (Glenn, 1992). Furthermore, not only does the exercise of power over women differ among men, but also among men and among women. For example, heterosexual men and women exercise greater power than gay men and lesbians, upper-class men and women greater power than working-class men and women, and white men and women greater power than men and women of color. Power, then, is a relationship that structures social interaction not only between women and men, but among men and among women as well. Notwithstanding, power is not absolute and, at times, may actually shift in relation to different axes of power and powerlessness. That is, in one situation a man may exercise power (i.e., as a patriarchal husband) whereas in another he may experience powerlessness (i.e., as a factory worker). Accordingly, masculinity and femininity can be understood only as fluid, relational, and situational constructs.

Connell's (1987, 1995a) notion of "hegemonic masculinity" and "emphasized femininity," the culturally idealized forms of masculinity and femininity in a given historical setting, is relevant here. Hegemonic masculinity and emphasized femininity are neither transhistorical nor transcultural, but vary from society to society and change within a particular society over time. In any specific time and place, then, hegemonic masculinity and emphasized femininity are culturally honored, glorified, and extolled at the symbolic level, such as the mass media, and are constructed in relation to subordinated masculinities and femininities (based on race, class, and sexual preference, for example), to oppositional masculinities and femininities, and to each other. In fact, hegemonic masculinity and emphasized femininity are the dominant forms of gender to which other types of masculinity and femininity are subordinated or opposed, not eliminated, and each provides the primary basis for relationships among men and among women as well as between men and women. In contemporary Western industrialized societies hegemonic masculinity currently is characterized by whiteness (race), work in the paid labor market (gender division of labor), the subordination of girls and women (gender relations of power), professional-managerial (class), and heterosexism (sexuality). Emphasized femininity is a form that complements hegemonic masculinity and is defined through not only similar characteristics such as whiteness and heterosexism, but also

> the display of sociability rather than technical competence, fragility in mating scenes, compliance with men's desire for titillation and ego-stroking [and] acceptance of marriage and child care. . . . At the mass level these are organized around themes of sexual receptivity in relation to younger women and motherhood in relation to older women. (Connell, 1987, p. 187)

In addition, then, to the gender, race, and class divisions of labor and power just discussed, sexuality is a major social structural feature of gender relations and, therefore, of the social construction of masculinities and femininities. Indeed, in Western industrialized societies a hierarchical system of sexual value exists, with marital-reproductive heterosexuals alone at the top, followed closely by unmarried heterosexuals, by those who prefer solitary sexuality, prostitutes, lesbians and gay men, transsexuals, transvestites, and sadomasochists (Rubin, 1984). Accordingly, heterosexuality is deemed normative, and "deviant" or subordinated sexualities are ridiculed, policed, and repressed. Not surprisingly, heterosexuality becomes a fundamental indication of "maleness" and "femaleness," gay masculinities and lesbian femininities are subordinated to heterosexual masculinities and femininities, and sexuality merges with other social structures to construct power relations among men and among women, such as the myth of the black rapist in relation to white and African American men.

Hegemonic masculinity and emphasized femininity, as the culturally dominant discourse, influences but does not determine masculine and feminine behavior. Hegemonic masculinity and emphasized femininity underpin the conventions applied in the enactment and reproduction of masculinities/femininities—the lived pattern of meanings, which as they are experienced as practices, appear as reciprocally confirming. As such, hegemonic masculine and emphasized feminine discourse shapes a sense of reality for most men and women, and is continually renewed, recreated, defended, and modified through practice. And yet, they are at times resisted, limited, altered, and challenged. As Barrie Thorne (1993, p. 106) notes: "Individuals and groups develop varied forms of accommodation, reinterpretation, and resistance to ideologically hegemonic patterns." Consequently, hegemonic masculinity and emphasized femininity operate as discourse that is "on hand" to be actualized into practice in a range of different circumstances. They provide a conceptual framework that is materialized in the design of social structures and, therefore, in daily practices and interactions.

Hegemonic masculinity and emphasized femininity, then, are more than simply the transmission of discourse that men and women can and do reproduce and challenge. In fact, at times and under certain social conditions, men and women construct "oppositional masculinities/femininities" that in one way or another are extrinsic to and represent significant breaks from hegemonic and emphasized forms, and may actually threaten their dominance. For example, various oppositional masculine practices, such as rejection of work in the paid labor market as significant to masculine identity, are constructed usually from subordinated race-and-class masculine conditions. Opposition, however, does not require such subordination. Indeed, increasing numbers of white, heterosexual, middle-class men are rejecting the notion of the subordination of women and attempting to construct egalitarian practices and relations with women. These profeminist men act against, and provide resistance to, certain aspects of hegemonic masculinity. Hegemonic and emphasized gender discourse, then, is not merely adaptive and incorporative; authentic transgressions within and beyond it occur under specific race-and-class social conditions.

The concepts "hegemonic/emphasized," "subordinated," and "oppositional" masculinities and femininities permit investigation of the different way men and women experience their everyday world from their particular positions in society and how they relate to other men and women. Although men and women attempt to express aspects of hegemonic/emphasized gender discourse through speech, dress, physical appearance, activities, and relationships with others, these social signs of masculinity and femininity are associated with the specific context of one's actions and are self-regulated within that context. Thus, masculinity and femininity are based on a social construct that reflects unique circumstances and relationships—a social construction that is renegotiated in each particular context. In other words, social actors self-regulate their behavior and make specific choices in specific contexts. As Connell (1987, p. 186) points out, everyday masculine and feminine practices draw on the cultural ideals of gender but do not correspond necessarily to actual masculinities and femininities as they are lived: What most men and women support is not necessarily what they are (p. 186). In this way, then, men and women construct varieties of masculinities and femininities through specific practices. By emphasizing diversity in gender constructions, we realize a more fluid and situated approach to our understanding gender.

Four Case Studies

This perspective permits us to conceptualize gender, race, class, and crime more realistically and completely, enables us to explore how and in what respects gender, race, and class are constituted in certain settings at certain times, and how each construct relates to various types of crime. The case studies that follow focus on explaining the differentiation of masculinities (Chapters 1, 2, and 4) and femininities (Chapter 3) by observing the work and product of their construction in specific social settings and through certain practices. Throughout,

I examine masculinities and femininities as they are reproduced among different races and classes. In my view, the definition and interpretation of the boundaries among masculinities and femininities, and thus the hierarchical separation of certain men and certain women from "Other" men and women, are critical to understanding crime in Western industrialized societies. Accordingly, the specific masculine and feminine meanings constructed through particular conceptions of race and class, and the way in which crime is related to those meanings and conceptions, must be analyzed. As such, I argue that only through analysis of *gender, race, and class in the making* can we make coherent sense of *the making of crime* at various times in history and under differing social situations.

Although men and women are always constructing gender, race, and class, the significance of each accomplishment is socially situated and, thus, is intermittent. That is, certain occasions present themselves as more effectively intimidating for demonstrating and affirming gender, race, and class. In such settings, specific categories are particularly salient; a time when "doing difference" (West & Fenstermaker, 1995) requires extra effort. Under such conditions, crime may be invoked as a means for constructing gender, race, and class. Consequently, in the case studies that follow, I examine the making of gender, race, class and crime under such conditions during selected historical time periods and in different social situations.

Chapter 1, Lynchers, examines the relationship among large-scale social change, racial masculinities, and lynching during Reconstruction and its immediate aftermath (1865-1900) in the U.S. South. Chapter 2, Hustler, undertakes a life-history study of the relationship among the social construction of race, class, masculinities, and crime in the life of Malcolm X. Chapter 3, Bad Girls, explores violence among lower working-class gang girls of color as a means of constructing a specific race and class femininity. Chapter 4, Murderous Managers, investigates the link between class and corporate masculinities among white managers and engineers involved in the decision to launch the space shuttle *Challenger*. Finally, the Epilogue, Summary Thoughts and Future Directions, offers suggestions for future academic work on the interrelation among gender, race, class, and crime from a structured-action perspective.

Notes

1. The first wave of the U.S. feminist movement traditionally dates from the abolitionist movement of the 1830s to the successful passage of the 19th Amendment (guaranteeing women the right to vote) in 1920.

2. For background on feminist theory in relation to crime and criminology, see Daly and Chesney-Lind, 1988 and Messerschmidt, 1993.

3. Unlike West and Fenstermaker (1995), in the "structured-action theory" presented here, both social structure and social action are key. I agree with Howard Winant's (1995, p. 504) recent criticism of West and Fenstermaker that their theory of "doing difference" misses the fact that "social structure must be understood as dynamic and reciprocal; it is not only a *product* of accreted and repeated subjective action but also *produces* subjects." This is consistent with my argument here and elsewhere (Messerschmidt, 1993) in which I follow the important theoretical insights of Giddens (1976, 1984) and Connell (1987, 1995a) that structure is realized only through social action and social action requires structure as its condition.

Chapter

Lynchers

In the 1924 edition of *Criminology*, Edwin Sutherland (1924, pp. 239-249) devoted 10 pages to the crime of lynching (the unlawful assault, killing, or both of an accused person by mob action). Sutherland (p. 239) was concerned especially with the fact that lynching, although occasionally employed during slavery, became a systematic event in the South between 1865 and 1900. Sutherland (pp. 242-243) offered two insightful and significant reasons for instantaneous white mob violence. The first, and to Sutherland (p. 242) the "underlying" reason, is "race prejudice or a feeling of white superiority." In particular, when African Americans were "emancipated" from their subordinate slave position, "great antagonism" by whites took the form of lynching (p. 242). Yet according to Sutherland (p. 243), lynching occurred for a second reason: as "compensation for the sex habits of white men in relation to negro women" (p. 243). Recognizing the widespread rape of African American women by white men, Sutherland (p. 243) continues, "The white woman must be shown to be infinitely different from the negro woman and lynching of the negro rapist is one way of doing this."

Through his seeming ability to transcend the intellectual climate of his time, Sutherland points to the importance of inequality in what today we call race relations (e.g., maintenance of white supremacy) and gender relations (e.g., sexuality, and its relation to masculinity and femininity). Clearly, Sutherland perceived the theoretical importance of race, gender, and sexuality to a proper understanding of lynching.[1] Although it is not surprising that Sutherland recognized the importance of "race prejudice," it is significant, and possibly surprising to many, that he underscores the "sex habits of white men" and their relation to African American and white women as well as the alleged "negro rapist." Yet this is as far as his thoughts reached and they demonstrate the limitations one would expect from pre-feminist work. The social and historical context in which Sutherland wrote embodied a relative absence of sociological/criminological theorizing on gender, race, sexuality, and crime.

Nevertheless, Sutherland was clearly on to something. Although asserting the importance of the "sex habits of white men" and their relation to the alleged "negro rapist" to understanding the phenomenon of lynching, no investigation of the relationship among gender, sexuality, and lynching has emerged in criminology. Indeed, the topic is ignored altogether in recent sociological/criminological accounts.[2]

In what follows, I take seriously Sutherland's assertion and argue that a complete understanding of lynching is possible only through a comprehension of the interrelation among race, masculinity, and sexuality. As argued later, during Reconstruction and its immediate aftermath, lynching was a response to the perceived erosion of white male dominance and was an attempt to recreate what white supremacist men imagined to be a lost status of unchallenged white masculine supremacy. Disguised in chivalric intimations, that is, as retribution for the alleged rape of a white woman by an African American man, lynching enforced white supremacy as well as gender hierarchies between men and women and among men. Thus, the specific masculine meanings constructed through particular conceptions of race and the way in which violence as practice is related to those meanings and conceptions are analyzed in this chapter. As such, I argue that only through analysis of *racial masculinities*, in particular, the social construction of white supremacist masculinity, can we make coherent sense of lynching and other forms of white male mob violence at this time in U.S. history.

Slavery

Slavery legally bound all blacks to the patriarchal "white father" and cut slaves off from all birthrights they may have enjoyed as members of a community. Male and female slaves were without social status or political and economic power; they could not own property, earn a living for themselves, or participate in public and political life. Slavery conveyed to all blacks that the fullness of humanity would never be available to them and overtly sought to reduce them to dependent, passive, childlike characters. In short, slavery produced a white supremacist discourse and practice that declared the physical, intellectual, and moral superiority of whites over blacks.

The master-slave relation constructed a masculine power hierarchy in which the "white master" was *the* representative of hegemonic masculinity. Indeed, powerful hegemonic masculinity was associated with white male supremacy, inasmuch as citizenship rights meant "manhood" rights that inhered to white males *only* (Bederman, 1995). Cultural ideology and discourse claimed that the most "advanced" races had evolved the most pronounced gender differences. A white "civilized" planter woman (the mistress) represented the highest level of womanhood—delicate, spiritual, exempt from heavy labor, ensconced in and dedicated to home. A white "civilized" planter man (the master) was the most manly creature ever evolved— firm of character and self-controlled, who provided for his family and steadfastly protected "his" woman and children from the rigors of the workaday world. Indeed, the symbols of hegemonic masculinity during slavery were whiteness; heading a heterosexual family; ownership of land, slaves, or both; literacy; and participation in political affairs. In particular, politics was extremely salient to white hegemonic masculinity in 19th-century U.S. slave society. Paula Baker (1984, p. 628) explains as follows:

> Parties and electoral politics united all white men, regardless of class or other differences, and provided entertainment, a definition of manhood, and the basis for a male ritual. Universal white manhood suffrage implied that because all [white] men shared the chance to participate in electoral politics, they possessed political equality. The right to vote was something important that [white] men held in common.

Participation in politics, then, was an essential practice for defining white men (hegemonic masculinity) in relation to black men (subordinate masculinity) and to all women. Indeed, political parties were fraternal organizations that bonded white men through their whiteness—it bound men to others like themselves. The notions of "womanhood" and "blackness" served as negative referents that united all white men. Politics, however, made gender and race the most significant divisions—white men saw beyond class differences and found common ground with other white men (Baker, 1984, p. 630). Participation in politics was an essential practice that triggered and consolidated racial and masculine identities; it was a resource for doing "white masculinity." Slavery institutionalized black men as "Other" and restricted male slaves from engaging in hegemonic masculine practices (Thorpe, 1967, p. 159). Because "whiteness" was the standard against which all else was measured, white men and white masculinity were constructed in contrast to subordinate "Other" men and "Other" masculinities.

Moreover, according to scientific and popular ideology, the "savage races" had not evolved the proper gender differences that whites possessed, and this is precisely what made them savage (Russett, 1989, pp. 130-155). Indeed, slavery denoted black males and females as more alike than different—"genderless as far as the slaveholders were concerned" (Davis, 1983, p. 5). In the middle of the 19th century, seven of eight slaves (men and women alike) were field workers, both profitable labor-units for the master. Predictably, black slaves did not construct the gender differences of the white planter class. The race and gender division of labor and power in slavery caused black women not to construct themselves as the "weaker sex" or the "housewife," and not to construct black men as the "family head" and the "family provider" (Davis, 1983, p. 8). Because "woman" was synonymous with "housewife" and "man" synonymous with "provider," the practices of black slaves could not conform to hegemonic gender ideologies and, therefore, were considered gender anomalies. In other words, black male slaves were defined as less than men and black female slaves less than women (Bederman, 1995, p. 20).

This construction of racial boundaries through gender also had its sexual component. White southerners differentiated themselves from "savages" by attributing to the latter a sexual nature that was more sensual, aggressive, and beastlike than that of whites. Influenced by the Elizabethan image of "the lusty Moor," white southerners embraced the notion that blacks were "lewd, lascivious, and wanton people" (D'Emilio & Freedman, 1988, p. 35). Both their gender similarity and animallike sexuality, white supremacist discourse declared, proved blacks were a subordinate species; therefore, it was natural that races must not mix and that whites must dominate blacks. Both scientific and popular thought supported the view that whites were civilized and rational, but that blacks were savage, irrational, and sensual (Jordan, 1968; Takaki, 1982). Indeed, it was this notion of race corporeality that defined inequality between whites and blacks and constructed what Frankenberg (1993) recently labeled an "essentialist racist discourse." Such a discourse constructs blacks as "fundamentally Other than white people: different, inferior, less civilized, less human, more animal, than whites" (p. 61). The articulation and deployment of essentialist racism as the dominant discourse for thinking about race marks the moment when race is constructed as *difference:* alleged white biological superiority justifies economic, political, and social inequalities in slavery.

Not surprising, social and legal regulations, such as prohibiting marriage between black men and white women, affecting interracial sexuality served to produce and cement racial identities. Slavery "heightened planter insistence on protecting white women and their family line, from the specter of interracial union" (D'Emilio & Freedman, 1988, p. 94). The commitment in slave society was protection of white female virtue and containment of white female sexuality within white, marital, reproductive relations (p. 95). In contrast to this draconian social control of white women,

> southern white men of the planter class enjoyed extreme sexual privilege. Most southern moralists condoned white men's gratification of lust, as long as they did so discreetly with poor white or black women. Polite society condemned the public discussion of illicit sex, but men's private writings reveal a good deal of comfort with the expression of pure sexual desire, unrelated to love or intimacy. (D'Emilio & Freedman, 1988, p. 95)

Indeed, rape of black female slaves by white masters rivaled separation of families as the most provocative event in black family life (Jones, 1986, p. 37). Slaves endured the daily pervasive fear that such assaults were possible, especially given the easy circumstances under which such rape could be committed. For example, one Louisiana master would enter the slave cabin and tell the husband "to go outside and wait 'til he do what he want to do." The black husband "had to do it and he couldn't do nothing 'bout it" (pp. 37-38). And Angela Davis (1983, pp. 23-24) points out that the practice was a weapon of domination and repression "whose covert goal was to extinguish slave women's will to resist, and in the process, demoralize their men." Indeed, sexual abuse of slave women in the presence of slave husbands/fathers made the point that slave men were not "real men" (Genovese, 1974, p. 482).[3] Thus, greater regulation of white women's sexuality was matched by greater sexual privilege for white men, and "provided white men with both a sexual outlet and a means of maintaining racial domination" (D'Emilio & Freedman, 1988, p. 94).[4]

Moreover, although denigration of interracial sexuality evoked the notion of virility, the sexually active black male as a threat to white women (Fox-Genovese, 1988, p. 291), this clearly was overshadowed by the social control of white female sexuality noted earlier. Indeed, as Elizabeth Fox-Genovese (p. 291) points out, "The presumed threat of black male sexuality never provoked the wild hysteria and violence in the Old South that it did in the New." Thus, although approximately 300 lynchings were recorded between 1840 and 1860, less than 10% involved blacks (the majority were white abolitionists). Black lynching was carried out primarily in the wake of an insurrection scare, not because of sexual liaisons with white women, and, therefore, were insignificant numerically prior to Emancipation (Genovese, 1974, p. 32).

Also, during slavery black men could be acquitted or pardoned for raping white women (Hodes, 1991). In slave society rape meant the rape of white women—for it was not a crime to rape black women. Consequently, when a black man raped a black woman he could be punished only by his master, not by the court system (Genovese, 1974, p. 33). Slaves accused of raping white women occasionally suffered lynching, but the vast majority were tried (Schwarz, 1988; Spindel, 1989). Indeed, during slavery mob violence was not the norm as a response to a charge of black-on-white rape but, rather, public policy left the matter in the hands of the courts (Genovese, 1974, p. 34). Moreover, not all rape trials resulted in conviction, and appellate courts in every Southern state

> threw out convictions for rape and attempted rape on every possible ground, including the purely technical. They overturned convictions because the indictments had not been drawn up properly, because the lower courts had based their convictions on possibly coerced confessions, or because the reputation of the white victim had not been admitted as evidence. (Genovese, 1974, p. 34)

The latter ground, the reputation of the *white* victim, is telling. For sexual conduct of slave men seemed to matter less to white southerners than did the sexual conduct of white women. White women who did not practice purity and chastity when unmarried and observe decorum when married were severely admonished (Fox-Genovese, 1988, pp. 235-236).[5] Indeed, the sexual reputation of the white woman was so important to the white community that even if the evidence was clear that a black-on-white rape did in fact occur, if the victim was of "bad character," the black rapist quite possibly would go free. James Hugo Johnston (1970, p. 258), in his study of miscegenation in the South from 1776-1860, was "astonished" at the number of rape cases in which

> white citizens of the communities in which these events transpired testify for the Negro and against the white woman and declare that the case is not a matter of rape, for the woman encouraged and consented to the act of the Negro.

The case of Carter, a "Negro man slave" in antebellum Virginia, and Catherine Brinal, the white female victim, is an excellent example (Johnston, 1970, pp. 259-260). Carter was found guilty of the rape of Brinal and sentenced to death. Yet the judge determined that Carter was the "proper object of mercy" because community members testified that Ms. Brinal

> was a woman of the worst fame, that her character was that of the most abandoned in as much as she (being a white woman) has three mulatto children, which by her own confession were begotten by different negro men; that from report she had permitted the said Carter to have peaceable sexual intercourse with her, before the time of his forcing her.

Consequently, this view of white female sexuality and the social control of that sexuality strongly outweighs the sexuality and social control of black men during slavery (Hodes, 1991, p. 41-42).

In sum, white slave masters and black male slaves constructed unique types of racial masculinity (hegemonic vs. subordinate) during slavery by occupying distinct locations within the particular race and gender divisions of labor and power. Both male groups experienced the everyday world from their proprietary positions in slave society and, consequently, there existed patterned ways in which race and masculinity were constructed and represented. Clearly, white and black men situationally accomplished masculinity in response to their socially structured circumstances.

Moreover, the meaning of "white masculinity" hinged on the existence of a subordinated "black masculinity."[6] Indeed, the power of white men rested on the racializing and sexualizing of masculinities. In slave society, hegemonic white masculinity was the standard against which all else was measured. Juxtaposed against the inherent "purity" and "goodness" that was white masculinity, black masculinity was essentially "impure" and "evil." This is notably evident in the sexualizing of masculinities because black masculine sexuality was constructed as animalistic and bestial. Nevertheless, despite an emphasis on the evil and threatening black masculine body and sexuality, in slave society the social control of white female sexuality received greater attention by white southerners than did black masculine sexuality.

Reformulating Black Masculinity

The passage of the 13th Amendment (1865) outlawed slavery; with emancipation former slaves became "African Amcricans." Through the process of Reconstruction (1865-1877), the Union attempted to restore relations with the Confederate states. Arguably the most crucial issue of Reconstruction was the political status of former black slaves as African Americans. As citizens, and, therefore, through changing practices in the community, family, economy, and politics, African Americans constructed gender in new ways that challenged white supremacy. Indeed, former slaves immediately began asserting independence from whites by forming churches, becoming politically active, strengthening family ties, and attempting to educate their children (Zinn, 1980, p. 195). In fact, emancipation was defined in terms of the ability of former slave men and women to fully participate in U.S. life. This meant not only acquiring citizenship rights as African Americans, but also living out the gender ideals hegemonic in U.S. society. In particular, for African American men, there was a euphoric desire to seize the rights and privileges of citizenship and, thereby, hegemonic masculinity.

As discussed earlier, under slavery black men were unable to construct hegemonic masculinity as economic "providers," as participants in social and political affairs, and their family authority ultimately was inferior to that of the white master. With emancipation, however, came developments that strengthened their authority within the African American family and institutionalized the notion that men and women should inhabit separate spheres. By 1870, the majority of African Americans lived in two-parent patriarchal family households, in which African Americans embraced the new "cult of domesticity," women worked primarily in household labor, and men became the public representative of the family.[7] African American former slave men now considered it a "badge of honor" for their wives to work at home, and thereby gained considerable power within the household (Foner, 1988, p. 86). To former slave men, the ability to support and protect a family was synonymous with manhood. Embracing this ideology, the Freedman's Bureau[8] appointed the husband as "head of the household," assigning to him sole power to enter into contractual labor agreements for the entire family. Moreover, the Freedman's Bureau Act of 1865 assigned the right for allotment of land only to males (women could claim land only if unmarried) (p. 87).[9] In short, the phenomenon of "separate spheres" as discourse for hegemonic masculinity and emphasized femininity provided the definitional space needed for gender practices by African Americans no longer denied the right to maintain family bonds (Wiegman, 1993).

The Reconstruction program contemplated that the freedom of African American men included the "natural" social superiority over African American women, and served to perpetuate gender divisions common in 19th-century U.S. society (Wiegman, 1993, p. 457). Thus, only African American men served as delegates to statewide organized constitutional conventions (held in 1867 and 1868) where they demanded equality with whites—from access to public education to the right to bear arms, serve on juries, establish newspapers, assemble peacefully, and enter all avenues of agriculture, commerce, and trade. And African American men were quite successful. Not only did they help write Southern state constitutions, but by 1868, African American men could serve on juries, vote, hold political office, and rise to political leadership (in the Republican party); African American women, like their white counterparts, could not (Foner, 1988, p. 87). Indeed, by 1869, former slave voting accounted for 2 African American members of the U.S. senate and 20 congressmen: 8 from South Carolina, 4 from North Carolina, 3 from Alabama, and one each from the other former Confederate states (Zinn, 1980, p. 195). Moreover, the 14th Amendment (ratified in 1868) declared that "all persons born or naturalized in the United States" were citizens and that

> no state shall make or enforce any law that shall abridge the privileges or immunities of citizens of the United States; nor shall any State deprive any person of life, liberty, or property, without due process of law; nor deny to any person within its jurisdiction the equal protection of the laws.

Also, in the late 1860s and early 1870s, Congress enacted several laws making it a crime to deprive African Americans of their rights and requiring federal officials to enforce those rights. These laws gave African Americans the right to contract and to buy property (Zinn, 1980, p. 194).

The move, then, from slavery to citizenry resulted in African Americans attempting to take control of conditions under which they labored, free themselves from economic and political subordination to white authority, and carve out the greatest possible measure of economic autonomy. Many African American men refused to continue working under the direction of an overseer and hundreds refused to sign labor contracts with their former masters (Foner, 1988, p. 105). Indeed, freedmen understood that their status after the war significantly depended on their economic status (Zinn, 1980, p. 192). Although many attempted to obtain some portion of the land they labored on, the vast majority of African American men, however, emerged from slavery landless—entering the free labor market as competitors with whites in the wage labor pool. Whereas freedmen attempted to organize their economic and political lives as independently as possible, they consistently faced racist obstacles.

Nevertheless, these new masculine practices by African American men in family, political, and economic relations represented not only the reformulation of black masculinity but the simultaneous loss of white masculine power. Under Reconstruction, exclusive white male control of politics, property, and family life ceases, thus creating a threatening situation for hegemonic white masculinity, and the result is a striking and extensive transformation of particular gender and race divisions of labor and power (Wiegman, 1993).

"Doing" White Supremacist Masculinity Through Lynching

Within the context of Emancipation, then, the race-and-gender social structures were altered profoundly. The African American emergence from slavery as citizens was characterized by a reformulation of gender and race divisions of labor and power and the simultaneous emergence of a new African American masculinity. In such a social setting, the definitions and practices outlining both race and masculinity were obscured and, as argued below, white male mob violence emerges as an attempt to forcibly reestablish the old meanings and hierarchy.

White male violence was immediate. For example, in May 1866, 46 African Americans were killed when their schools and churches were burned by a white male mob in Memphis; in July of the same year, 34 African Americans were killed in New Orleans by a white mob (Ayers, 1984, p. 161).

In general, the violence against African Americans was conducted by assorted cabals of white males. Of course, one of the largest of these was the Ku Klux Klan (KKK), which was organized in 1865 by six young returning Confederate officers as a secret social "club" in Pulaski, Tennessee (Foner, 1988, pp. 425-444, 454-459; Trelease, 1971, pp. 3-27). The activities of the organization soon embraced the harassment of freed people, and "club" branches were established throughout the South in 1868 (Trelease, 1971, p. 64).

Klan membership, as with other white male mobs during this period, included men of all classes of white Southerners, with leadership usually drawn from the more well-to-do (Dowd Hall, 1979, pp. 132, 139-140; Rable, 1984, p. 30). Of most concern to white supremacist males was the equation of African American male social practices with manhood. Indeed, conduct deemed "manly" by white men (such as involvement in politics) came to exemplify "insolence" and "insubordination" when practiced by African American men. African American men who engaged in any practice defining a masculinity that indicated they were "acting like a white man" became appropriate subjects for white male violence. As Rable (1984, p. 92) put it, the Klan "was especially sensitive" to African American male practices that challenged white male power.

Although African American women and whites who supported the rights of African American men were also victims of terror, the greatest violence was reserved for African American men who engaged in such "improper" masculine practices. Accordingly, African American men who were politically active (e.g., voting Republican, becoming a member of the Republican Party, or both), who displayed economic independence (e.g., owning property, doing well economically, or both), or who violated face-to-face boundaries of the masculine color line (e.g., "talking back" to a white man) were the major targets of white male violence (*"The Condition of Affairs,"* 1871). Moreover, these alleged "improper" masculine practices often were coupled with any conduct that could be construed as a threatening sexual overture toward white women (Hodes, 1991).

The violence directed against such masculine practices ranged from whippings, to lynching, to castration. For example, in 1869, approximately 20 KKK men raided the home of Aaron Biggerstaff, an African American man politically active in the South Carolina Republican Party, and severely whipped him. According to testimony given to the Joint Select Committee on the Condition of Affairs in the Late Insurrectionary States[10] (*"The Condition of Affairs,"* 1871, Pt. 2, pp. 213, 584), Biggerstaff "was whipped for being too intimate with some white women" *and* "for being a leading Republican."

The case of Jourdan Ware (Pt. 6, pp. 44-45, 66-67, 74-75, 885, 920), an African American man assaulted and later murdered by Klansmen in northwest Georgia in 1870, is another example of the emerging concern of white supremacist men over African American masculine practices. Ware was considered "a prominent man among the colored people," and the assault to have been "on account of his politics" and "to break him up" economically. In other words, Ware was assaulted because he was "too political" and "fixed very comfortably." Moreover, in addition to his political activities and economic independence, Ware engaged in other "improper" masculine practices. For instance, Ware was considered to be "a big, mighty forward, pompous negro" who was "impudent" toward white men; "he pushed about among white men too much." "He made an insulting remark to a white lady"; he allegedly stated: " 'How d'ye sis,' as the young lady passed down the road. He called her 'wife' and thrust his tongue out at her. The lady ran away very frightened." The eventual killing of Ware was justified by the Klan because "the lady was spared the mortification and shame of appearing in court in connection with a cause that the delicacy of any lady would shrink from in terror."

The case of Henry Lowther presents yet another example of white supremacist male concern with political, economic, and sexual independence of African American men. Lowther was a 40-year-old ex-slave in Georgia who in 1870 was both a member of the Republican Party and was economically independent. Lowther was arrested for conspiracy to commit murder and, at 2 a.m. one morning, approximately 180 Klansmen came to the jail and carried off Lowther to a swamp. Lowther explained to the Joint Select Committee (*The Condition of Affairs*, 1871, Pt. 6, p. 357) what happened next:

> Every man cocked his gun and looked right at me. I thought they were going to shoot me, and leave me right there. The moon was shining bright, and I could see them. I was satisfied they were going to kill me, and I did not care much then. Then they asked me whether I preferred to be altered or to be killed. I said I preferred to be altered.

After castrating him, the Klansmen left Lowther in the swamp to bleed to death. He made it home, however, and survived to recount the violence to the Committee. Asked by the Committee why the Klan came to the jail for him, Lowther (*The Condition of Affairs,* 1871, Pt. 6, pp. 359, 362) gave three reasons:

They said that no such man as me should live there . . . I worked for my
money and carried on a shop. They have been working at me ever
since I have been free. I had too much money.

They said I had taken too great a stand against them in the Republican
Party.

They said I was going to see a white lady.

Similarly, in 1870 ex-slave Bill Brigan was taken from his home
by the Klan on suspicion of involvement with white women in
Georgia; Brigan was "tied down on a log and they took a buggy-trace
to him, and whipped one of his seeds [testicles] entirely out and the
other nearly out" (*"The Condition of Affairs,"* 1871, Pt. 6, p. 359).

How can we begin to make sense of such white male mob violence
directed primarily toward African American men exhibiting political,
economic, and sexual independence? Under the social contract of
Emancipation, African American male participation in the politi-
cal/economic arena as competitors threatened white masculine status.
The "invasion" of African American men into these critical hegemonic
masculine spheres posed a very real threat to white men's monopoly
over politics and jobs; one way to discourage such competition and
reestablish racial and masculine meanings and practices was to use
violence to remind African American men of their subordinate "Oth-
erness." In other words, white men secured both a specific type of
"whiteness" and "maleness" by emphasizing the subordinate status of
African American male competitors. The meaning of white supremacist masculinity is defined through the collective practice of lynching.
Indeed, mob violence helped white supremacist men define who they
were by directing hostility toward African American men as a symbol
of what they were not. In the particular social context of emancipation, African American male accountability to race and sex categories
is called into play. Politically and economically independent African
American men confound the possibility of differentiating men according to race and, therefore, undermines the legitimacy of white male
supremacy. Whippings, lynchings, and castrations conveyed to African American men that white men were ready to punish the slightest
deviation from tolerated lines of their "subordinate masculinity."

When African American men dared step over the lines, they were made examples of what was acceptable and of what was expected from the entire race (Harris, 1984, p. 19).

Although not all white males engaged in such violence, the unique social setting of Emancipation, as example of large-scale social change, increased the likelihood of this particular type of violence because white supremacist masculinity was "explicitly put on the line" (Morgan, 1992, p. 47). It was critical that mob violence be seen as communicating indignation against African American men for invading a white male bastion, and for threatening the economic and social status of white men.

Indeed, under slavery political participation and economic independence was an ideal arena for differentiating racial masculinities; engaging in these activities demonstrated clearly that players were "white" and "real men." Thus, in the Reconstruction South, African American males engaging in the same activities diluted this masculine and race distinction: If African American men were permitted to do what "real men" (white men) did, the value of the practice to accomplishing white masculinity was effectively compromised. And because part of "doing gender" means creating racial differences and, therefore, racial boundaries among men, by maintaining and emphasizing the subordinate status of African American men through violence, white men were attempting to restore those distinctions and, thus, to preserve the peculiarity of white supremacist masculinity. Mob violence served to solidify, strengthen, and validate white supremacist masculinity and simultaneously to exclude, disparage, and subordinate African American masculinity. Indeed, it reinforced the commonality of white males as against the pernicious "Other."

Finally, what the case illustrations reveal is a heightened and intense white male concern with every interaction between white women and African American men, especially if it indicated even the slightest possibility of interracial sexuality. In other words, under conditions of Emancipation, attention to relationships between white women and African American men was intensified. Indeed, the African American male had joined with the white female as *the* major targets of sexual regulation. It is to this regulation that we now turn.

Race, Sexuality, and the Chivalric Phallacy

Most chroniclers of lynching say little about lynchings that occurred during Reconstruction (most examine lynching from the late 1880s). Those who do, however, found that "the practice was widespread" (Rable, 1984, p. 98). Richard Maxwell Brown (1975, pp. 214, 323) writes that from 1868 through 1871, the Klan engaged in large-scale lynching of African American men. Indeed, he records over 400 Klan lynchings of African Americans in the South over this time: 291 in 1868, 31 in 1869, 34 in 1870, and 53 in 1871. Similarly, George C. Wright (1990, pp. 41-42) reports in his study of Kentucky that more than one third of the lynchings that occurred in that state (117 of 353) happened between 1865 and 1874, "with 2 years alone, 1868 (with 21) and 1870 (with 36), accounting for the extremely high number of 57."

Moreover, in the 1880s and 1890s, the number of lynchings gradually increased (but never reached the 1868 level). During those years, the heyday occurred in the early 1890s, when the largest number of African American lynchings occurred in 1892 (106; Tolnay & Beck, 1995, p. 271).

The vast majority of victims during this period (1882-1900) were charged with alleged sexual offenses with white women (Brundage, 1993, p. 263; Tolnay & Beck, 1995, p. 49). Indeed, as Brundage (1993, p. 58) reports in his study of lynching from 1880 to 1930, "white Southerners maintained that rape was the key to lynching" whether or not a rape actually occurred. Rape became such an elastic concept within the white community during Reconstruction and its immediate aftermath that it stretched far beyond the legal definition to include "acts as apparently innocent as a nudge" (p. 61). For example:

> On November 8, 1889, a mob lynched Orion Anderson in Loudoun County, Virginia, for an alleged attempted "assault" of a 15-year-old white girl. In fact, the black youth, a friend of the girl, had merely donned a sack on his head and frightened her while she walked to school. (Brundage, 1993, p. 61)

Perhaps more telling, the following event illustrates the intense white supremacist male interest in sexuality between white women and African American men. When a 16-year-old white girl became pregnant by her African American male lover, the girl's father had the African American male

> promptly arrested for rape even though the girl adamantly refused to accuse him. While he was being transported to the county jail, a mob seized him and hanged him. The tragic affair ended when the young girl committed suicide by taking an overdose of sleeping pills. (Brundage, 1993, p. 62)

In addition, lynchings for any such interaction suggesting interracial sexuality increasingly included sexual mutilation (Dowd Hall, 1979, 1983). As Brown (1975, p. 151) shows, "the lynching of Southern blacks routinely came to be accompanied by the emasculation of males." Indeed, the typical lynching became a white community celebration, with men, women, and children cheering on the mutilation and hanging, burning, or both, at the stake. As Raper (1969, p. 12) shows, white women spectators figured prominently in the ordeal, inciting "the men to do their 'manly duty' " and "inspiring the mobs to greater brutalities."

The lynching process extended for several hours, during which the African American male suffered excruciating pain from torture, mutilation, and castration committed throughout the ordeal by certain white supremacist males. The finale featured spectator scavenging for "souvenirs" of African American body parts (Brown, 1975, pp. 217-218).

The 1899 lynching of Sam Holt in Newman, Georgia provides an effective example (Ginzburg, 1988, pp. 11-14). Holt was charged and detained for the alleged rape of a white woman. Soon a mob of whites gathered outside the jail, and the Sheriff of the town "turned the negro over to the waiting crowd" (p. 13). Although the alleged rape victim "was not permitted to identify the negro" because "it was thought the shock would be too great for her," a procession quickly formed and the doomed marched at the head of the shouting crowd (approximately 2,000 white people) down several streets (pp. 11,

13). Eventually a tree was chosen, and Holt was tied from a branch facing the crowd. Immediately his clothes were torn from him and a heavy chain was wound around his body. The local press reported what happened next:

> Before the torch was applied to the pyre, the negro was deprived of his ears, fingers, and genital parts of his body. He pleaded pitifully for his life while the mutilation was going on, but stood the ordeal of the fire with surprising fortitude. Before the body was cool, it was cut into pieces, the bones were crushed into small bits, and even the tree on which the wretch met his fate was torn up and disposed of as "souvenirs." The negro's heart was cut into several pieces, as was also his liver. (Ginzburg, 1988, p. 12)

None of the white male lynchers attempted to disguise their appearance and there was no effort to prevent anyone from seeing who lighted the fire or mutilated and castrated the body. On the contrary, there was a festival atmosphere. Finally, on the trunk of a nearby tree was pinned a placard that read: "We Must Protect Our Southern Women."

Under Emancipation, African American male sexuality, viewed as dangerous and animallike, grew to become an even greater threat assiduously waiting to be unleashed. By opposing this embodiment of evil, white supremacist men affirmed their version of morality and virtue, while at the same time their status as white men. Lynching reconstructs African American men as "natural" "animalistic" rapists; by resolutely and "bravely" avenging the alleged rape of pure white womanhood, Southern white men framed themselves as chivalric patriarchs, avengers, and righteous protectors (Dowd Hall, 1983, p. 335).

As demonstrated, hegemonic white male masculinity was measured by the ability to control, provide for, and protect his home—especially the white woman at the center of it. Under conditions of Emancipation, interracial sexuality represented the loss of all this. Thus, when a white man acted to save "his woman" from the bestial African American male, he constructed himself as savior, father, and keeper of racial purity (Harris, 1984, p. 20). White women were regarded as being at risk and had to be protected in the name of the race. By this commitment, then, white men taught "their women" that there was nothing to fear by capturing the source of that fear, tor- turing it, and killing it (p. 20). In this way, white supremacist men regained patriarchal hegemonic masculine status by determining what was wrong with society, ferreting it out, and reestablishing the norm as it existed before the interruption (p. 20). Lynching for rape up- held white privilege and underpinned the objectified figure of white women defined as "ours" and protected by "us" from "them" (Fraiman, 1994, p. 73). These beliefs formed what Fraiman (p. 73) calls the white male chivalric phallacy—preservation of white mascu- line supremacy was refigured as protection of white females for white males. Over and over again Klan members and other white suprema- cists told the Joint Select Committee (*"The Condition of Affairs,"* 1871, Pt. 2, pp. 364, 399, 422) that "females shall ever be special objects of our regard and protection." Using her emblem as the keeper of racial purity, these white men cast themselves as protectors of civilization, thereby reaffirming not only their role as social and familial "heads," but their paternal property rights as well (Wiegman, 1993, p. 461). In this view, interracial sexuality destroyed what it meant to be a man because white masculinity was inextricably tied to race: To be a man was to be a white man who had sole access to and the duty to protect white women. The lynching and castrating of African American men, founded on the protection of white women, was central to securing white male power and identity and, therefore, reconstructing a hierarchal masculine difference between white and African American men.

Moreover, in the context of the 19th-century feminist movement, the necessity for disrupting potential bonds between white women and African American men was critical (Wiegman, 1993). The women's movement challenged hegemonic white masculinity by agi- tating for female access to activities traditionally reserved for men, in particular white men, from economic to political equality. For exam- ple, during Reconstruction Susan B. Anthony and Elizabeth Cady Stanton founded not only the National Woman Suffrage Association but also *The Revolution*, which became one of the best-known independent women's newspapers of its time. The motto of the weekly paper was: "Men, their rights and nothing more; women, their rights and nothing less." In addition to discussions of suffrage, *The Revolution* critically examined topics ranging from marriage to sexuality.[11]

It was also during the 1870s and 1880s that the "New Woman" appeared in U.S. society (Smith-Rosenberg, 1985, p. 26). The New Woman was single, highly educated, and economically autonomous; she eschewed marriage, fought for professional visibility, and often espoused innovative and radical economic and social reforms (p. 245). As Smith-Rosenberg (p. 245) shows, the New Woman "challenged existing gender relations and the distribution of power" and, therefore, "challenged men in ways her mother never did." Indeed, according to Michael Kimmel (1987, p. 270), one white male response to this visible and outspoken feminist movement, as well as to the New Woman, was "to push women out of the public domain and return them to the home as passive, idealized figurines."[12]

Kimmel (1987), however, overlooks the response of lynching and castrating African American men. Violence against alleged "black rapists" earned white men positions of superiority over white women as well as over African American men; thus lynching equated with the preservation of race via passive white femininity. The lynching scenario constructed white women as frail, vulnerable, and wholly dependent for protection on chivalric white men. In this way, lynching and the mythology of the "black rapist" reproduced race and gender hierarchies during a time when those very hierarchies were threatened by both the New Woman and the "New Man" (African American male). Protection of white women reinforced femaleness and thus the notion of "separate spheres," while simultaneously constructing racial boundaries between white and African American men (Harris, 1984, p. 19). Lynching, then, was a white male resource for "doing difference" (West & Fenstermaker, 1995) between men and women and among men. Accordingly, lynching the mythic "black rapist" not only constructed African American men as subordinate to white men, but simultaneously perpetuated the notion of separate spheres and inequality between white men and white women.

Yet, this still leaves unanswered the reason for castrating African American males in public spectacles. Arguably, the increased reliance on public castration made clear the profound white supremacist male distress over masculine equality and similarity with African American men. As Robin Wiegman (1993, p. 450) eloquently puts it:

> Within the context of white supremacy, we must understand this threat of a masculine sameness as so terrifying that only the reassertion of a gender difference can provide the necessary disavowal. It is this that lynching and castration offer in their ritualized deployment, functioning as both a refusal and a negation of the possibility of extending the privileges of patriarchy to the black man.

Both race and masculine differences were reproduced through the practice of lynching and castration by ultimately emasculating the African American male body. African American masculine equality and similarity was discredited symbolically through publicly displayed castrated bodies. Possible sameness with white men was compromised violently in favor of continued primacy of white masculine supremacy (Wiegman, 1993); the practice of lynching and castration provided a resource for the physical enactment of white masculine hegemony. Indeed, in phallocentric culture, the penis becomes the phallus through the embodiment of generative gendered power. Thus, for African American men, movement from slave to citizen encompassed this symbolic exchange between penis and phallus (p. 449). And as Wiegman (pp. 449, 465) concludes, "castration circumvents this process of exchange, consigning the black male to the fragmented and decidedly feminized realm of the body," while simultaneously the white male retains "hegemony over the entire field of masculine entitlements."[13]

Conclusion

Reconstruction created the social context for constructing an alarmist ideology about African American male sexuality and the resulting pronounced public mob violence employed by white supremacist men. White supremacist men bonded into lynching mobs that provided arenas for an individual to prove himself a white man among white men. During Reconstruction and its immediate aftermath, gender and race became extraordinarily salient and, thus, white supremacist men developed strong ties with their neighbors, their acquaintances, and with those whom they perceived to be like themselves. In particular, participation in mob violence demonstrated that one was a "real white man." Within the social context of the white male mob, this hegemonic white supremacist masculinity is sustained by means of collective practices that subordinate African American men and, therefore, a specific African American masculinity. Indeed, the individual "style" of the white male mob member is somewhat meaningless outside the group; it is the lynching mob that provides meaning and currency for this type of white masculinity. White supremacist men, then, were "doing" a specific type of whiteness and masculinity simultaneously as they were "doing" lynching; "doing" race, gender, and lynching merged into one entity. The collective struggle for supremacy over African American men was a means with which to gain recognition and reward for one's white masculinity, and a means with which to solve the gender and race problems of accountability. Mob violence was a situational resource for surmounting a perceived threat by reasserting the social dominance of white men. Lynching the "bestial black rapist" reconstructed racial masculinities in hierarchical terms of essential, biological inequality. In short, these white supremacist men gained status, reputation, and self-respect through participation in mob lynchings, which symbolically, especially through the ritual of castration, disclaimed an African American male's rights to citizenry, freedom, and self-determination.

Notes

1. Sutherland (1924, pp. 242-243) had several other reasons for lynching, which included the "exhilaration" lynching produced in an unexciting South and the "weakness" of the courts and police.

2. Although Sutherland (1924) can be excused for not developing further his ideas on gender, sexuality, and lynching, recent sociological work on the topic has no such excuse. For example, a recent book on

lynching, Tolnay and Beck's (1995) *A Festival of Violence,* renders gender and sexuality completely invisible.

3. Nevertheless, slave men often attempted to protect slave women from such violence. As Jacqueline Jones (1986, p. 37) shows, the literature is "replete with accounts of slave husbands who intervened at the risk of their own lives to save wives and children from violence at the hands of whites."

4. Anne Firor Scott (1970, pp. 54-55) argues that many white women found this sexual double standard difficult to accept, and engaged in premarital and extramarital affairs.

5. Indeed, throughout the North and South during this time period the largest proportion of women arrested were charged with such "moral misbehavior" as adultery, fornication, and bastardy (Spindel, 1989, pp. 82-86).

6. Both slave men and free blacks recognized this purported subordinate masculinity. A central theme of the abolitionists' attack on slavery was that it robbed black men of their manhood. And male slaves who agitated for freedom demanded their "manhood rights," equating freedom and equality with manhood (Horton, 1993, pp. 83-85). Moreover, black men who enlisted in the Union Army and fought in the Civil War conceptualized the practice as marking a watershed in the construction of "true" black masculinity. As Cullen (1992, p. 77) found in his examination, exhibiting "real manhood surfaces again and again as an aspiration, a concern, or a fact of life" for these black soldiers.

7. Because African Americans were involved increasingly in sharecropping, however, it became necessary for African American women to contribute to family income. Thus, a "separate spheres" ideology was at best a temporary phenomenon (Foner, 1988, p. 86).

8. In March 1865, Congress created the Freedman's Bureau to protect the interests of African Americans in the South, and to help them obtain jobs and establish African American hospitals and churches.

9. Many African American women resisted this forced patriarchal component of African American family life (Foner, 1988, p. 88).

10. In 1871, Congress appointed a joint committee to investigate violence against African Americans in the former Confederate states. Witnesses testified that throughout the late 1860s white male terrorism was directed primarily against politically active and economically independent African American men, who refused to defer to white supremacists, engaged in any conduct that indicated a possible sexual liaison with white women,

or both. This government document is one of the few primary sources on white mob violence during Reconstruction.

11. For an informative account of the racism inherent in this "first wave" of the feminist movement, see Davis (1983, pp. 46-86).

12. In addition to this antifeminist response, Kimmel (1987, pp. 269-277) outlines two additional responses by men: a "masculinist" response that urged a greater participation by men in the rearing of boys and a "profeminist" response that embraced feminist principles as a solution to this crisis of masculinity.

13. The legacy of this racist violence has been extensive "legal lynchings" by the state. For example, between 1930 and 1967, 455 men were executed for rape in the United States; 405 were African American men and all victims of the convicted rapists were white women (Wolfgang & Riedel, 1975). Moreover, a number of these cases have proven to be "miscarriages of justice" in which innocent men were executed (Bedau & Radelet, 1987).

Chapter

Hustler

In Chapter 1, I examined the relationship among large-scale social change, racial masculinities, and collective violence at a specific time and place in U.S. history. Chapter 2 shifts the analysis from the collective to the individual. Here I examine the life of Malcolm X as documented in one of the most significant works of the 20th century, *The Autobiography of Malcolm X* (Malcolm X, 1964). The life-history perspective is particularly relevant because it richly documents personal gendered experiences and transformations over time. Indeed, a life history records "the relation between the social conditions that determine practice and the future social world that practice brings into being" (Connell, 1995a, p. 89).

Moreover, there is a long and illustrious criminological tradition of life history as a source for studying crime (Bennett, 1981; Sampson

& Laub, 1993). Such classics of criminology as Clifford Shaw's (1930) *The Jack-Roller* and Edwin Sutherland's (1937) *The Professional Thief* illustrate, as Sampson and Laub (1993, p. 204) recently declared, "the power of life-history data to illuminate the complex processes of criminal offending."

In analytically examining the life of Malcolm X, however, Chapter 2 departs from all earlier criminological life-history studies by concentrating on the relationship between masculinities and crime at selected pivotal moments in Malcolm's development from childhood to adulthood. The chapter focuses on the process through which Malcolm X constructed various masculinities in specific race and class social contexts, how crime is employed to produce and sustain a specific race and class masculine identity at a certain point in his history, and how Malcolm X eventually desists and refrains from crime by reformulating his masculinity.

The life-history perspective, then, affords us the opportunity to examine how certain masculine practices underpin crime in specific social situations and relationships (gender, race, and class), evidencing how these masculinities are accomplished through criminal practices. In essence, Chapter 2 emphasizes evolving gender, race, and class conditions; varieties of masculinities; and movement in and out of crime in the life of one individual—Malcolm X.[1]

Malcolm Little

Malcolm X was born Malcolm Little in Omaha, Nebraska on May 19, 1925. Most of Malcolm's early life was spent in and about Lansing, Michigan. His family moved to Lansing from Omaha because of an attack on the Little home by Ku Klux Klan nightriders in early 1925 (Malcolm X, 1964, p. 1). The attack was a racist response to his father's political activities as a Baptist minister and dedicated organizer for Marcus Garvey's United Negro Improvement Association (UNIA), a nationalist "back-to-Africa" movement of the 1920s.

Among Malcolm's (Malcolm X, 1964) most vivid childhood memories of Lansing is an incident that occurred in 1929 when he was about 4 years old:

> I remember being suddenly snatched awake into a frightening
> confusion of pistol shots and shouting and smoke flames. My father
> had shouted and shot at the two white men who had set the fire and
> were running away. Our home was burning down around us. (p. 3)

The Little home was burned to the ground by the "Black Legionnaires," a white supremacist mob who had been threatening Reverend
Little because he wanted to open a store and live outside the "Negro
district"—in other words, he was "acting like a white man." Following the loss of their home, the Little family moved to a farm 2 miles
outside Lansing.

In addition to early memories of white racism, Malcolm's memories of family interaction reveal a patriarchal gender division of labor and power. Child care and household duties were assigned to
Malcolm's mother: "My mother . . . seemed to be always working—
cooking, washing, ironing, cleaning, and fussing over us eight children" (Malcolm X, 1964, p. 7). Malcolm's father was the power
figure in the home who "provided for the family" and who devoted
his life to the Garvey movement. Malcolm (Malcolm X, 1964, p. 6)
recognized early on the significance of such activities to his developing sense of masculinity:

> I knew that the collections my father got for his preaching were
> mainly what fed and clothed us, and he also did other odd jobs, but
> still the image of him that made me proudest was his crusading and
> militant campaigning with the words of Marcus Garvey. As young
> as I was then, I knew from what I overheard that my father was
> saying something that made him a "tough" man. I remember an old
> lady, grinning and saying to my father, "You're scaring these white
> folks to death!"

Malcolm also recalls conflict between his mother and father that
frequently resulted in violence. As Malcolm put it (Malcolm X, 1964,
p. 4): "They seemed to be nearly always at odds. Sometimes my father
would beat her."[2] Malcolm's father also "savagely" beat the older
children if they broke any of his rules, and "he had so many rules it
was hard to know them all" (p. 4). Thus, underpinning the management of the Little home was a gendered structure of authority and

power that secured Reverend Little's position as "head of the household."

Similarly, Malcolm's older brothers and his older sister influenced his gender development in important ways. For example, after his father was killed by Black Legionnaires (beaten unconscious and thrown in front of a train), his oldest sister, Hilda, "attended to the babies," while his oldest brother, Wilfred, entered the wage-labor market (Malcolm X, 1964, p. 11):

> He quietly quit school and went to town in search of work. He took any kind of job he could find and he would come home, dog-tired, in the evenings, and give whatever he had to my mother.

Clearly, through this interaction with his mother, his father, his sister, and his brother Malcolm grew up with *un*ambiguous definitions of "doing gender": men's work versus women's work (at home and in the workplace) and who, ultimately, has authority and power over others.

Predictably, when Joe Louis knocked out James Braddock in 1937 to become the heavyweight champion of the world, "every Negro boy old enough to walk wanted to be the next Brown Bomber" (Malcolm X, 1964, p. 23). Malcolm's brother Philbert was no exception, and indeed was praised by many in the community as a "natural boxer." Malcolm frequently would go to the gym and watch Philbert train, "It was very exciting. Perhaps without realizing it I became secretly envious" (p. 23). Indeed, Malcolm attempted to emulate his brother. In his very first bout, however, he was knocked down 50 times by a "white boy" in front of his brothers and sisters, as well as "just about everyone else I knew in town" (p. 23). This masculine "failure," according to Malcolm (p. 24)

> did such a job on my reputation in the Negro neighborhood that I practically went into hiding. A Negro just can't be whipped by somebody white and return with his head up to the neighborhood.[3]

Malcolm's brother Philbert, like his other brother Wilfred and his father, was what masculinity "was all about." And Malcolm's attempt at boxing undertook to practice what was being preached and represented. Connell (1995a, p. 122) defines this proactive adoption of "family values" as the "moment of engagement" with hegemonic masculinity, "the moment in which the boy takes up the project of hegemonic masculinity as his own."

The death of Reverend Little drove Malcolm's family further into poverty by worsening economic conditions and ongoing racist/sexist discrimination, which limited the economic options available to Malcolm's mother. Under the harsh Depression conditions of the 1930s, Malcolm's mother failed to maintain her sanity, was institutionalized in a mental hospital, and the children, including Malcolm, were made "wards of the state."

Each child was placed in a foster home, and at age 13 Malcolm came under the custodial control of a white couple, the Swerlins, of Mason, Michigan. This was Malcolm's first close relationship with white people; in retrospect, he notes that "they were good people" (Malcolm X, 1964, p. 26). Although the Swerlins also "liked" Malcolm, they refused to consider him a human being. Rather, they looked on him as a "mascot," a family pet. As Malcolm (p. 26) put it:

> They all liked my attitude, and it was out of their liking for me that I soon became accepted by them—as a mascot. They would talk about anything and everything with me standing right there hearing them, the same way people would talk freely in front of a pet canary. They would even talk about me, or about "niggers," as though I wasn't there, as if I wouldn't understand what the word meant. A hundred times a day, they used the word "nigger."

Malcolm remained in the Swerlins home through the eighth grade, and was an active and successful student at predominantly white Mason Junior High School. Malcolm was very popular and, as he states (Malcolm X, 1964, p. 28): "It became hard for me to get through the school day without someone after me to join this or head up that—the debating society, the junior high basketball team, or some other extracurricular activity. I never turned them down."

Although family and school relations provided ample support for Malcolm's continued engagement with hegemonic masculinity, his masculine construction simultaneously occurred within the context of white racism. As Malcolm states (Malcolm X, 1964, p. 31), he responded to white racism by constructing an accommodating masculinity. Indeed, at this particular time he aspired to becoming a *white male:*

> In the second semester of the seventh grade I was elected class president. It surprised me even more than other people. But I can see now why the class might have done it. My grades were among the highest in the school. I was unique in my class, like a pink poodle. And I was proud; I'm not going to say I wasn't. In fact, by then, I didn't really have much feeling about being a Negro, because I was trying so hard, in every way I could, to be white.

Within the social settings of a white household and a white junior high school, Malcolm accomplished gender through conformance to school rules and participation in student organizations, reflecting wholehearted adoption of the school and its overall enterprise. Because masculinity is a behavioral response to the particular conditions and situations in which we participate, Malcolm was doing masculinity within the home and school in a specific way. The challenge for Malcolm was to produce configurations of masculine behavior that could be seen as normative by others in his immediate social milieu. Accordingly, Malcolm developed a controlled and cooperative gender strategy of action for institutional success. Malcolm's agenda, simply, was to become an accomplice to the institutional order. Therefore, Malcolm constructed gendered actions in relation to how such actions might be interpreted by others (their accountability) in the particular social context in which they occurred.

But Malcolm's serious attempt at integration, as he later put it, was upset in the eighth grade when "something happened that was to become the first major turning point in my life" (Malcolm X, 1964, p. 35). His English teacher asked him whether he had been thinking about a career. Malcolm (p. 36) responded as follows:

> "Well, yes sir, I've been thinking I'd like to be a lawyer." Mr. Ostrowski looked surprised, I remember, and leaned back in his chair and clasped his hands behind his head. He kind of half-smiled

and said, "Malcolm, one of life's first needs is for us to be realistic . . . you've got to be realistic about being a nigger. You need to think about something you *can* be."

Because of this interaction, the reality of long-standing racist attacks on Malcolm's humanity became obvious. He grew despondent and drew back from white people. "Where 'nigger' had slipped off my back before, wherever I heard it now, I stopped and looked at whoever said it" (Malcolm X, 1964, p. 37). In short, from this moment on, Malcolm distanced himself from what had been to this point an accepted race and gender framework.

After completing the eighth grade, Malcolm asked to be transferred to the custody of his half-sister Ella, who lived in Boston, Massachusetts. The change of custody was approved, and Malcolm moved from Lansing to Boston. As he states, "No physical move in my life has been more pivotal or profound in its repercussions" (Malcolm X, 1964, p. 38).

Detroit Red

Ella lived in the middle-class "Hill" section of Roxbury, a part of Boston in which African Americans were "allowed" to live. There existed sharp class distinctions between the "Hill Negroes" of Ella's neighborhood and the Roxbury working class "town people." These distinctions resulted in serious class tensions, such that African American middle-class members found it necessary to distinguish themselves from the "Black commoners" in order to increase "their class and status differentiation for integration with whites" (Tyler, 1989, p. 37). Thus, Roxbury's middle-class African Americans promoted "manners, morals, and dress codes" that conformed to white middle-class standards (p. 37).

As a drugstore fountain clerk two blocks from Ella's house, Malcolm (Malcolm X, 1964, p. 59) found it increasingly difficult to "serve up sodas, sundaes, splits, shakes, and all the rest of that fountain stuff to those fancy-acting Negroes." Malcolm (p. 59) continues: "I couldn't stand those Hill characters . . . those penny-ante squares who came in there putting on their millionaires' airs, the young ones and old ones both, only annoyed me." Thus Malcolm was more and more attracted to the ghetto street life than to Ella's middle-class Roxbury society. Indeed, it was the "cool cats" who mostly attracted Malcolm's attention. As he states (p. 43):

> I spent my first month in town with my mouth hanging open. The sharp-dressed young "cats" who hung on the corners and in the poolrooms, bars and restaurants, and who obviously didn't work anywhere, completely entranced me.

A friend he met at one of the poolrooms, "Shorty," got him a job as a shoeshine boy at the Roseland Ballroom, which rapidly became the center of his social life. In fact, it didn't take long for Malcolm to learn that the job required less shoe shining than "selling liquor and reefers, and putting white 'Johns' in touch with Negro whores" (Malcolm X, 1964, p. 49).

Street culture attracted Malcolm not only because of his developing class consciousness, and, therefore, opposition to the "Hill Negro" lifestyle, but because of his experiences with exclusion and white hostility in Lansing (his developing race consciousness). Malcolm had found a new locale that seemed more amiable and inviting. He began to "hang out" at night with Shorty and his friends, who taught him the pleasures and practices of a "hipster" lifestyle. Eventually he adopted the stellar masculine social sign of this culture—a "zoot suit" consisting of "sky-blue pants 30 inches in the knee and angle-narrowed down to 12 inches at the bottom, and a long coat that pinched my waist and flared out below my knees" (Malcolm X, 1964, pp. 52-54). Malcolm added a narrow leather belt with his initial "L" (for Little) on it; a blue hat with a feather in the 4-inch brim; and a long, thick-linked, gold-plated chain that swung down lower than his coat hem. He also acquired a "fire-red conk" (straightening of the hair). And so Malcolm became a practicing member of the zoot suit masculine culture.

By the late 1930s, the term *zoot* was common currency within urban jazz culture; it defined something worn or performed in an extravagant style. Because many young African American males wore suits with padded shoulders and trousers that were tapered at the ankles, the term *zoot suit* passed into everyday usage (Cosgrove, 1984, p. 40). Moreover, the zoot suit became *the* display of those negotiating a specific masculine, race, and class identity. As Cosgrove (p. 40) states, "the zoot suit was a refusal: a subcultural gesture that refused to concede to the manners of subservience." Zoot-suiters were young African American men who refused to integrate with white society, frequently dodged the draft, and rejected African American middle-class "respectability." Furthermore, zoot-suiters challenged, at the symbolic level, essentialist notions of gender, race, and class. In fact, they represented what Dick Hebdige (1978, p. 89) calls an "interference," rendering problematic how gender, race, and class traditionally are defined and practiced. Zoot-suiters mocked the normality of inequality and opened "the world to new readings" (p. 102). Rather than concealing their oppression, zoot-suiters "flaunted their difference" (Cosgrove, 1984, p. 41). Disengaging themselves from whites and middle-class African Americans, zoot-suiters collectively constructed a specific race-and-class identity, centering on a "opposition hipster masculinity."[4]

With straightened hair[5] and zoot suit, Malcolm began to spend most of his free time at the Roseland, where he fell in love with the lindy-hop and eventually quit his shoe shine job to devote more time to dancing. Indeed, he couldn't wait to leave the "hill clowns" where Ella lived to "get dressed in my zoot and head for some of my friends' places in town, to lindy-hop and get high, or something, for relief from those hill clowns" (Malcolm X, 1964, pp. 59-60).

Malcolm found a collective identity in the zoot suit culture—a feeling of belonging after rejection in Lansing and a sense of power-lessness and separation in middle-class African American culture. Coincidentally, the zoot-suiter culture provided a collective public challenge to the white supremacist definition of African American as "Other." Malcolm found much of this collective identity, and sense of potency and purpose acted out in the Roseland (Malcolm X, 1964, p. 49):

They'd jam-pack that ballroom, the black girls in way-out silk and satin dresses and shoes, their hair done in all kinds of styles, the

men sharp in their zoot suits and crazy conks, and everybody grin-
ning and greased and gassed.

Social interaction at, for instance, Boston's Roseland Ballroom
afforded working-class African Americans to be something distinct
from the "Other." The Roseland provided a stronghold in which
African Americans could experience a sense of control over their lives
denied them elsewhere. For working-class African Americans, who
daily endured back-breaking wage labor, low income, long hours, and
pervasive racism, places like the Roseland were places to "take back
their bodies"—part of a subaltern culture that underscored pleasure,
marginalized work as the primary signifier of self, and celebrated a
working-class racial identity (Kelley, 1992, p. 163). Rather than
deferentially accepting their structured destiny, they constructed collective practices to oppose and counter such oppression.

In the thick of the Roseland crowd, Malcolm delighted in observing "the real Roxbury hipsters eyeing my zoot and fine women giving
me that look" (Malcolm X, 1964, p. 58). And, in the collective zoot
suit atmosphere, Malcolm constructed this "opposition masculinity"
that must be seen in relation to subordinate types of masculinity
within the same setting. For example, one evening at the Roseland,
Malcolm (p. 58) passed his shoe shine replacement,

> a scared, narrow-faced, hungry-looking little brown-skinned fellow
> just in town from Kansas City. And when he recognized me, he
> couldn't keep down his admiration and wonder. I told him to "keep
> cool," that he'd soon catch on to the happenings. Everything felt
> right when I went into the ballroom.

The "sharp" look and demeanor of zoot-suiters were partly intended to upstage other men in the masculine-dominated arena of the
street where they earn applause for their "style." As Steve Chibnall
(1985, p. 60) put it, "the imposing machismo of the sharp black dude
was a source of an almost charismatic appeal in the search for identity
of the young." Zoot-suiters literally pranced above nonzoot-suiters,
thereby constructing a specific race and class loftiness of masculinity.
In other words, gender, race, and class were largely constructed

and presented through a collective stylistic strategy and, therefore, Malcolm's individual practices represented part of "the lived dynamics of inequality" (Ferrell, 1995, p. 182).

The same evening Malcolm (Malcolm X, 1964, pp. 66-67) subordinated his shoe shine replacement, he met a white woman, Sophia, and describes the meeting in the following way:

> In any black ghetto in America, to have a white woman who wasn't a known, common whore was, for the average black man, at least, a status symbol of the first order. And this one, standing there, eyeing me, was almost too fine to believe. Shoulder-length hair, well built, and her clothes had cost somebody plenty. . . . She didn't dance well, at least not by Negro standards. But who cared? I could feel the staring eyes of other couples around us.

Indeed, it was Sophia at his side that helped provide Malcolm (p. 68) with increased masculine status:

> It was when I began to be seen around town with Sophia that I really began to mature into some real status in black downtown Roxbury. Up to then I had been just another among all of the conked and zooted youngsters. But now, with the best looking white woman who ever walked in those bars and clubs, and with her giving me the money I spent, too, even the big, important black hustlers and "smart boys"—the club managers, name gamblers, numbers bankers, and others—were clapping me on the back, setting us up to drinks at special tables.

Confirming and locating his sexuality in relation to the other "cool cats" was for Malcolm a resource for doing masculinity. Masculine definitions of women in the zoot suit culture contributed greatly to Malcolm's heterosexual male identity and, according to Kelley (1992, p. 170), wealthy white women ranked higher than African American women in zoot suit culture. Moreover, unlike African American women, white women

> belonged to "Charlie," the "Man," "whitey," and were theoretically off limits. Thus, in a world where most relationships were commod-

ified, white women, in the eyes of hustlers at least, were regarded as stolen property, booty seized from the ultimate hustle. (Kelley, 1992, p. 170)

Eventually, Malcolm moved out of Ella's house to share an apartment with Shorty and to obtain a new job. When the United States entered World War II, Malcolm was 16 and too young for service; however, by lying about his age he got a job on the railroad, the war having caused a shortage of African American porters, cooks, and waiters. Working on the "Yankee Clipper" from Boston to New York, Malcolm saw New York for the first time. During stopovers, Malcolm would "hang out" in Harlem where he "drank liquor, smoked marijuana, painted the Big Apple red with increasing numbers of friends" and, finally, "in Mrs. Fisher's rooming house" he caught "a few hours of sleep before the 'Yankee Clipper' rolled again" (Malcolm X, 1964, p. 78). Clearly, the zoot suit culture had become the mainstay of Malcolm's gender, race, and class identity.

In time Malcolm quit the railroad, moved to Harlem, and waited tables at Small's Paradise, a famous Harlem club, where he met the elite of Harlem's hustlers. Through interaction with Small's customers, Malcolm (Malcolm X, 1964, p. 83) was educated in the art of hustling:

> Every day I listened raptly to customers who felt like talking, and it added to my education. My ears soaked it up like sponges when one of them . . . would tell me inside things about the particular form of hustling that he pursued as a way of life. I was thus schooled well, by experts in such hustles as the numbers, pimping, con games of many kinds, peddling dope, and thievery of all sorts, including armed robbery.

When Malcolm had been in Harlem long enough to demonstrate "signs of permanence," he earned a nickname—"Detroit Red." Because most folks in Harlem had never heard of Lansing, when Malcolm was asked where he came from, he always mentioned Detroit. And so, with his "fire-red conk," he became known as Detroit Red.

Eventually, Detroit Red began hustling drugs to escape dependency on low-wage, menial labor. He states (Malcolm X, 1964, p. 99) the following:

> I kept turning over my profit, increasing my supplies, and I sold reefers like a wild man. I scarcely slept; I was wherever musicians congregated. A roll of money was in my pocket. Every day, I cleared at least 50 or 60 dollars. In those days (or for that matter these days), this was a fortune to a 17-year-old Negro. I felt, for the first time in my life, that great feeling of *free!* Suddenly, now, I was the peer of the other young hustlers I had admired.

Detroit Red was in the process of constructing a "hustler" opposition masculinity that entailed refusing to allow "legitimate work" to become the primary signifier of identity, privileging of leisure, and emphasizing "fast money" involving little or no physical labor (Kelley, 1992). Kelley (pp. 168-169) points out how this opposition masculinity differs from hegemonic masculinity in that possessing "capital" is not the ultimate goal of a hustler; rather, money is a means by which hustlers can avoid wage labor and engineer status through the purchase of prestigious commodities. In other words, the "hipster" "hustled" "fast money" to "lindy-hop until he was 'beat to the socks'" (Chibnall, 1985, p. 59).

The "zoot suit hipster hustler" clearly represented a specialized means with which to transcend race and class domination. Yet it also demonstrated the socially constrained nature of social action and how African American zoot-suiters reworked the hegemonic masculine discourse as a vehicle for achieving that transcendence. The challenge for Detroit Red was to construct forms of masculine behavior that could be seen as conventional by others in his immediate race and class milieu. Accordingly, Detroit Red developed criminal practices that permitted him to reject legitimate work and to privilege "fast money" and leisure. Detroit Red constructed gender, race, and class practices in relation to how such actions might be interpreted by others (their accountability) in the particular social context of the zoot suit African American culture. Moreover, this is consistent with the recent Ferrell and Sanders (1995a, p. 5) argument that the "subtleties

of collective style define the meaning of crime for subcultural participants" and, in turn, "the meaning of criminality is anchored in the
style of collective practice." Clearly, Detroit Red's criminality incorporated and reflected dimensions, meanings, and style of this zoot
suit culture.

Detroit Red now considered himself a "true hustler," "nervy and
cunning enough to live by my wits" (Malcolm X, 1964, p. 108). He
began to carry a .38 pistol and to do "stickup" (Katz, 1988). Doing
stickup was a means not only for obtaining "fast money"—it was
simultaneously a practice for doing masculinity (Malcolm X, 1964,
p. 109):

> I saw how when the eyes stared at the big black hole, the faces fell
> slack and the mouths sagged open. And when I spoke, the people
> seemed to hear as though they were far away, and they would do
> whatever I asked.

Robbery demonstrated he was in control. Indeed, a hustler must
always outsmart others. Detroit Red (Malcolm X, 1964, p. 127) put
it this way:

> For a hustler in our sidewalk jungle world, "face" and "honor" were
> important. No hustler could have it known that he'd been "hyped,"
> meaning outsmarted or made a fool of. And worse, a hustler could
> never afford to have it demonstrated that he could be bluffed, that
> he could be frightened by a threat, that he lacked nerve.

Robbery provided Detroit Red with a public ceremony of domination and humiliation of others. Participating in a social environment
where gender accountability is augmented, Detroit Red took part in
crimes that involved actual or possible confrontation with others. As
such, robbery provided an available resource with which to accomplish gender and, therefore, to construct a "hustler" masculinity—to
court danger and, through force of will, to subject others to it while
simultaneously obtaining "fast money." Doing stickup was doing
masculinity by manufacturing *"an angle of moral superiority* over the
intended victim" and, thereby, succeeding "in making a fool of his

victim" (Katz, 1988, pp. 169, 174). Moreover, survival in this dangerous atmosphere demonstrated to himself as well as to others the fierceness of his will; survival substantiated that he could "transcend the control of the system" (p. 231). Within the social context that Detroit Red participated, robbery was a rational practice for doing masculinity and for providing the funds necessary to support masculine accomplishment in the zoot suit culture.

After a time, and a narrow scrape with the police, Detroit Red fled back to Boston. There he formed a burglary ring with Sophia, her sister, Shorty, and his friend, Rudy. As Malcolm (Malcolm X, 1964, p. 142) later points out, the group was organized in a traditional gender division of labor:

> At our gang's first meeting in the apartment, we discussed how we were going to work. The girls would get into houses to case them by ringing bells and saying they were saleswomen, poll-takers, college girls making a survey, or anything else suitable. Once in the houses, they would get around as much as they could without attracting attention. Then, back, they would report what special valuables they had seen, and where. They would draw the layout for Shorty, Rudy, and me. The three men would then go, two of us to do the job while the third kept watch in the getaway car, with the motor running.

They would complete a burglary, "lay low awhile, living it up," and then burglarize again (Malcolm X, 1964, p. 145).

Clearly, gender is a situated accomplishment in which we produce forms of behavior seen by others in the same immediate situation as masculine or feminine. Within the confines and social setting of the burglary ring, Detroit Red and his friends simultaneously were doing burglary and gender. In other words, when women and men in the burglary ring "do" this division of labor, they simultaneously accomplish gender. The burglary ring became the engine that situationally produced "fast money" as well as gender in terms of difference. The result was a gendered burglary ring in which the men and women did masculinity and femininity in distinct ways. Eventually, however, they were all caught, and Detroit Red, not quite 21 years old, was sentenced to ten years in prison (p. 151).

Before moving on, it is important to note that in the process of attempting to transcend oppressive social structures, Detroit Red ultimately reproduced them. His zoot suit masculine style clearly defied specific forms of race and class conventionality, yet simultaneously was reactionary and reproductive of the gendered social order. In essence, Detroit Red (like other African American hipster hustlers) responded in a gender-specific manner to race and class oppression, which in turn locked him into the very structured constraints he attempted to overcome. Thus, zoot suit hustling became a form of social action that ultimately reproduced gender divisions of labor and power as well as normative heterosexuality.

Malcolm X

During his years in prison (1946-1952), Malcolm underwent significant change. He was influenced greatly by a prisoner named Bimbi, a self-educated man who convinced Malcolm of the value of education. Bimbi would lecture fellow prisoners on a variety of topics. As Malcolm (Malcolm X, 1964, p. 153) states: "He would have a cluster of people riveted, often on odd subjects you never would think of." During the years since leaving the eighth grade, Malcolm had forgotten how to read and write, but with Bimbi's tutelage and encouragement he began to read and study, even taking correspondence courses.

In 1948, one of Malcolm's brothers visited him in prison. Reginald told Malcolm that he had to get him out of prison. Reginald would not elaborate on his scheme, but he did tell Malcolm not to eat any more pork or smoke cigarettes. Purely on faith, Malcolm followed Reginald's advice. Reginald's plan was to enlist Malcolm in the Nation of Islam, the dominant African American nationalist movement of the period (Marable, 1991). This religious movement, taken over by Elijah Muhammad (1897-1975) in the 1930s, strongly urged separation of the races and considered the "white man" the devil incarnate—a tenet that Malcolm was, by this time, quite willing and eager to believe. Indeed, as Malcolm (Malcolm X, 1964, p. 161) states:

[Reginald] left me rocking with some of the first serious thoughts I had ever had in my life: that the white man was fast losing his power to oppress and exploit the dark world; that the dark world was starting to rise to rule the world again, as it had before; that the white man's world was on the way down, it was on the way out.

Reginald urged Malcolm to accept the teachings of Elijah Muhammad, which Malcolm readily did—as did thousands of young men in prison who were recruited into the Nation of Islam during this period. As Marable (1991, p. 56) shows, under Muhammad's leadership, the Nation of Islam recruited and transformed the most oppressed members of the race: convicts, dope addicts, pimps, young delinquents, prostitutes, criminals, and the permanently unemployed.

Moreover, the Nation of Islam further triggered Malcolm's passions by, in particular, challenging white supremacy. The Nation of Islam was part of the emerging civil rights movement that transformed conceptions of racial difference (Frankenberg, 1993, pp. 13-14). Essentialist racism was the benchmark against which oppositional discourses on race were articulated (Frankenberg, 1993, p. 139). Thus, the Nation of Islam insisted on difference but in a form distinct from essentialist racism—inequality results not from biology but from white supremacy. The themes were explicit (Pinkney, 1976, pp. 157-158):

1. We believe this is the time in history for the separation of so-called Negroes and the so-called white Americans.
2. We believe in justice for all, whether in God or not; we believe as others, that we are due equal justice as human beings.
3. We believe that the offer of integration is hypocritical and is made by those who are trying to deceive black peoples into believing that their 400-year-old open enemies of freedom, justice, and equality are, all of a sudden, their "friends."
4. We believe our women should be respected and protected as the women of other nationalities are respected and protected.

Regarding theme 4, when Malcolm was a member, the Nation of Islam was heavily male-dominated. The typical temple congregation of the 1950s was predominantly male (up to 80%), ranging in age from 17 to 35, and men appropriated the dominant positions in the affairs of the temples, with women holding honored but secondary positions (Collins, 1992, p. 76). Moreover, women's subordinate status included the following restrictions (Pinkney, 1976, p. 161):

> Women are forbidden to wear provocative or revealing clothing. They may not enter a room with a man to whom they are not married. They are expected to cook, sew, clean the living quarters, and care for their husbands and children.

These themes provided Malcolm (Malcolm X, 1964, p. 163) a more stable patriarchal masculine discourse, a challenge to white supremacy, and an immediate transformation:

> Every instinct of the ghetto jungle streets, every hustling fox and criminal wolf instinct in me, which would have scoffed at and rejected anything else, was struck numb. It was as though all of that life merely was back there, without any remaining effect, or influence. . . . The very enormity of my previous life's guilt prepared me to accept the truth.

The combination of Nation of Islam political ideology and personal events (such as early schooling and family experiences, his father's political thought and practice, and constant reference to negative experience with the hustling lifestyle) was sufficient to launch Malcolm on a program of reform. The venture called for a separation from the "hustler masculinity" and construction of a new "Muslim masculinity." Indeed, renunciation and denial of the validity of hustling provided the space in which new masculine qualities and practices could grow. Malcolm was still responding to race and class powerlessness, but with a new agenda and a new focus on race. He was now reformulating opposition masculinity within the context of specific race protest. That is, confined to the walled refuge of prison, where living the "fast life" did not constitute a resource for doing masculinity, he remained dedicated to certain aspects of hegemonic masculinity (e.g., heterosexuality, provide and protect the family, subordination of women) but his identity now reflected a new and explicit emphasis on the African American separatist struggle. This then represented a new and pivotal moment in the ongoing social evolution of Malcolm's various masculinities and race identities.

Malcolm (Malcolm X, 1964, p. 169) wrote to Elijah Muhammad, who wrote back welcoming him to the faith and stating that "the black prisoner symbolized white society's crime of keeping black men oppressed and deprived and ignorant, and unable to get decent jobs, turning them into criminals." Not long after this, Malcolm (p. 173) became a "prison hermit," spending most of his time reading:

> In every free moment I had, if I was not reading in the library, I was reading on my bunk. You couldn't have gotten me out of books with a wedge. Between Mr. Muhammad's teachings, my correspondence, my visitors . . . and my reading of books, months passed without my even thinking about being imprisoned. In fact, up to then, I never had been so truly free in my life.

The teachings of Elijah Muhammad stressed how history had been "whitened." This stimulated Malcolm's interest, particularly in the "glorious history of the black man." Malcolm (Malcolm X, 1964, p. 174) states: "I took special pains to hunt in the library for books that would inform me on details about black history." Through studying history he found compelling evidence of the white man's evil nature. Indeed, as Malcolm (pp. 176, 178) states:

> Book after book showed me how the white man had brought upon the world's black, brown, red, and yellow peoples every variety of the sufferings of exploitation. . . . Mr. Muhammad, to whom I was writing daily, had no idea what a new world had opened up to me through my efforts to document his teachings in books.

The myriad histories of non-Western civilizations confirmed Malcolm's new-found pride in his blackness. Indeed, it was "right there in prison that I made up my mind to devote the rest of my life to telling the white man about himself—or die" (Malcolm X, 1964, pp. 184-185). Race and gender had now become the two most telling features of Malcolm's life and, thus, he constructed a new type of race and masculine identity.

In 1952, Malcolm was paroled and left for Detroit to live with a brother, Wilfred, also a member of the Nation of Islam. His first purchases on leaving prison were a pair of glasses, a suitcase, and a wristwatch; Malcolm reasoned that these items symbolized his new identity. He began work in the furniture store that Wilfred managed— a job that reconfirmed white exploitation of African Americans (p. 193):

> In all my years in the streets, I'd been looking at the exploitation that for the first time I really saw and understood. Now I watched brothers entwining themselves in the economic clutches of the white man who went home every night with another bag of money drained out of the ghetto. I saw that the money, instead of helping the black man, was going to help enrich these white merchants, who usually lived in an "exclusive" area where a black man had better not get caught unless he worked there for somebody white.

Malcolm (Malcolm X, 1964, pp. 194-195) attended the same Temple as his brother Wilfred's family, and describes the gendered demeanor of Temple members:

> The men were quietly, tastefully dressed. The women wore ankle-length gowns, no makeup, and scarves covered their heads. The neat children were mannerly not only to adults but to other children as well. . . . I had never dreamed of anything like that atmosphere among black people who had learned to be proud they were black, who had learned to love other black people instead of being jealous and suspicious. I thrilled to how we Muslim men used both hands to grasp a black brother's both hands, voicing and smiling our happiness to meet him again. The Muslim sisters, both married and single, were given an honor and respect that I'd never seen black men give to their women, and it felt wonderful to me. The salutations that we all exchanged were warm, filled with mutual respect and dignity: "Brother" . . . "Sister" . . . "Ma'am" . . . "Sir." Even children speaking to other children used these terms. Beautiful!

Malcolm (Malcolm X, 1964, p. 199) eventually was formally inducted into the Nation of Islam, and changed his name from Malcolm Little to Malcolm X:

> The Muslim's "X" symbolized the true African family name that he never could know. For me, my "X" replaced the white slave-master name of "Little" which some blue-eyed devil named Little had imposed upon my paternal forebears.

Malcolm went to Chicago to meet Elijah Muhammad, eventually quitting his job to study personally under Muhammad—whom Malcolm considered his "savior." As Malcolm (Malcolm X, 1964, pp. 199, 205) states:

> I worshipped him. . . . The way we were with each other, it would make me think of Socrates on the streets of the Athens market place, spreading his wisdom to his students. Or how one of those students, Aristotle, had his students following behind him, walking through the Lyceum.

In 1953, Malcolm was appointed a Muslim minister, and returned to Boston to organize a Black Muslim temple. In 1954, he was posted to Philadelphia. As a reward for his speed and diligence in organizing the Philadelphia temple, he was appointed minister of Temple No. 7 in Harlem.

In the years between 1953 and 1963, the Nation of Islam grew from a small number of storefront temples to a large, organized, and vocal national movement dedicated to African American separatism— and Malcolm became its best-known and most volatile spokesperson. Malcolm evinced not simply a vibrant, earthly, and human character, but was a revolutionary "organic" teacher who displayed "total love for the dispossessed" (Marable, 1991, p. 87).

During this time, Malcolm continued as minister of Temple No. 7, and organized several other temples throughout the country. And he grew increasingly close to Elijah Muhammad, both as adviser and friend. As Malcolm (Malcolm X, 1964, p. 210) states:

> I have pledged on my knees to Allah to tell the white man about his
> crimes and the black man the true teachings of our Honorable Elijah
> Muhammad. I don't care if it costs my life.

Early in 1958, Malcolm married Betty X, a member of his Harlem
congregation. Over the next seven years they had four daughters:
Attilah, Qubilah, Ilyasah, and Amiliah. In this family setting, Malcolm
practiced the Nation of Islam's gendered theme outlined earlier.
Indeed, Malcolm (Malcolm X, 1964, p. 226) believed that

> the true nature of man is to be strong, and a woman's true nature
> is to be weak, and while a man must at all times respect his woman,
> at the same time he needs to understand that he must control her if
> he expects to get her respect.

To be sure, a patriarchal gender division of labor and power pre-
vailed within the X household—Malcolm the breadwinner/decision
maker and Betty the homemaker/caretaker. Moreover, Malcolm
clearly exercised power at home and further defined the household
setting in his terms. Indeed, Betty's ability to chart the course of her
life was subordinated to that of Malcolm.[6]

In this now more stable "nuclear-family" social setting, Malcolm
constructed a masculinity based solely on providing, monogamy, and
domination and control of women. Accordingly, as the social setting
changed, from the street and zoot suit culture to the political struggle
and "family man," so did Malcolm's conceptualization of normative
masculine and race behavior. Different social settings generate different masculinities (as well as race and class identities) and, in this case,
facilitate movement out of crime.[7] Malcolm was producing configurations of masculine behavior that could be seen by others in his
immediate social milieu, Temple members and family members, as
normative. And so, Malcolm constructed gendered actions in response to how such actions might be interpreted by others (their
accountability) in the specific social context in which they occurred.
This helps explain Malcolm's (Malcolm X, 1964, p. 170) surprise at
his new-found masculinity:

I still marvel at how swiftly my previous life's thinking pattern slid away from me, like snow off a roof. It is as though someone else I knew of had lived by hustling and crime. I would be startled to catch myself thinking in a remote way of my earlier self as another person.

Conclusion

The structure of the gender, race, and class divisions of labor and power and normative heterosexuality impinge on the construction of masculinity and crime. These structural features both preclude and permit certain resources that Malcolm used to pursue a gender strategy and to construct masculinities. The salience of gender, race, and class at various stages of Malcolm's life differed; the significance of each relation shifted with a changing social context. The choices made by Malcolm at each stage, and the resources available to carry out those choices, developed in response to the specific social circumstances in which he found himself.

Chapter 2 has attempted to demonstrate that Malcolm X produced specific configurations of behavior that could be seen by others in each immediate social setting of his life as masculine. These different masculinities emerged from practices that used different resources, and race and class relationships structured the resources available to construct specific masculinities. "Malcolm Little," "Detroit Red," and "Malcolm X" represented situationally accomplished, unique masculinities (e.g., hegemonic vs. oppositional) by drawing on different resources and discourses indigenous to their distinct historical position.

The focus here has been on the changes in Malcolm's masculine, race, and class identity within a range of social contexts: a childhood in which he was constantly battling to be accepted as a young man; a zoot suit culture where he was accepted as a "hipster" and "hustler" without stigma; and finally a spiritual and political movement in which he was celebrated as a father, husband, and national spokesperson. Across these sites and through a shifting currency of his sense of self-identity as a man (as well as a member of a race and class), Malcolm moved in and out of crime. Crime was appropriated as a resource for "doing" a unique type of race and class masculinity at a specific moment in his life, a time when gender, race, and class were extraordinarily significant. Understanding the complex construction of masculinities over time adds insight to our ongoing comprehension of movement into and desistance from crime. Indeed, in the social situation of prison and eventually the Nation of Islam, gender and race were particularly salient and facilitated "drift" out of crime. In short, crime as a resource for doing masculinity, race, and class changes over time and is situated in specific social contexts.

Notes

1. It was Thomas and Znaniecki (1958, pp. 1832-1833) who argued in their classic work *The Polish Peasant in Europe and America*, that "personal life records . . . constitute the *perfect* type of sociological material." The reason for such a claim is that autobiographical material provides rich detail of how individuals make sense of their world and the ways they interpret their own lives. Nevertheless, critics argue that autobiographical data represents a selective account of life events from the perspective of both subject and researcher. Thus, mindful of this criticism, I attempt to minimize "forcing the data" by employing what Plummer (1983, p. 114) calls "systematic thematic analysis" in which both theoretical framework and Malcolm's account interact to construct his gendered life history.

2. In retrospect, Malcolm (Malcolm X, 1964, p. 4) tended to blame his mother for the violence: "It might have had something to do with the fact that my mother had a pretty good education. . . . But an educated woman, I suppose, can't resist the temptation to correct an uneducated man. Every now and then, when she put those smooth words on him, he would grab her."

3. Michael Messner's (1995, pp. 109-110) important research on the relationship among race, class, masculinity, and sports points to a heightened community recognition of athletic ability as masculine validation in African American working-class neighborhoods.

4. Around the same time period, "pachuco" Chicano youth participated in a similar zoot suit opposition culture in the U.S. southwest (see Cosgrove, 1984; Turner & Surace, 1956).

5. The "conk" was not an attempt to look white but rather a refusal to "look like either the dominant, stereotyped image of the Southern migrant or the black bourgeoisie" (Kelley, 1992, p. 161).

6. In a recent interview, Betty X (Taylor & Edwards, 1992, pp. 107-109) revealed the following:

> I thought Malcolm was a little too strict with me. For example, he didn't want me to associate with anyone. He just wanted me to be for him. He didn't even want me to have women friends. . . . He was possessive from the beginning to end. . . . All my stress was over the fact that I wanted to work, and he wouldn't even entertain the idea. He didn't want anybody to have any influence over me that would in any way compete with his.

7. This is consistent with "social control" literature that persistently finds that "strong job stability and marital attachment reduce the likelihood of involvement in criminal behavior" (Sampson & Laub, 1993, p. 240). What social control literature eschews, however, is any comprehension of the important relationship between job stability and marriage as alternative resources for doing masculinity. In other words, although it consistently reports the correlation, it fails to explain it!

3

Bad Girls

In a recent attempt to develop a framework for explaining gendered crime, Darrell Steffensmeier and Emilie Allan (1991, p. 73) argue that men and women differ significantly in their "moral development," and that "women's moral choices" constrain them from behavior that could be harmful to others. Because women are "bound more intimately into a network of interpersonal ties, their moral decisions are more influenced by empathy and compassion" and this "ethic of care" constructs nonviolence and "suggests that serious predatory crime is outside women's moral boundaries."

Steffensmeier and Allan (1991) ignore the fact that there exists no "scholarship that demonstrates that the greater conformity of women is a function of their special virtues" (Naffine, 1987, p. 133).

But beyond this, are females always empathetic and compassionate? In such an analysis, we are hard put to explain the following by a member of the Turban Queens, a "girl" gang in New York City (Campbell, 1984/1991, p. 262):

> But once you're in a fight, you just think—you've got to fuck that girl up before she does it to you. You've got to really blow off on her. You just play it crazy. That's when they get scared of you. It's true—you feel proud when you see a girl you fucked up. Her face is all scratched or she got a black eye, you say, "Damn, I beat the shit out of that girl, you know."

Such violence becomes incomprehensible in an analysis that concentrates exclusively on sex differences. Departures from what is considered "appropriate female crime" are either ignored—indeed, there is a dearth of theorizing about female violence in criminological theory—or are deviantized as inappropriate at best, "masculine" at worst. For example, in the 1970s, Freda Adler (1975, p. 15) argued that because of the women's movement, women were becoming more masculine, resulting in an increasing number of women using "weapons and wits to establish themselves as full human beings, as capable of violence and aggression as any man." For Adler (1977, p. 101), because of "liberation" the " 'second sex' had risen" by the mid-1970s and, therefore, women became increasingly aggressive, violent, and masculine. Such a view defines, for example, the member of the Turban Queens quoted here as simply defective and freakish, not authentically female. Moreover, because criminology does not possess the theoretical language capable of representing violence by women, criminologists like Adler simplistically perceive women's violence from the perspective of violent acts by men. As Margaret Shaw (1995, p. 122) argues, the criminological image of violence by women "is based on that of male violence—macho, tough, aggressive; we have no ways of conceptualizing violence by women except in terms of its 'unnaturalness.' " Thus, criminology lacks theory that does not belittle women and punish them intellectually for stepping beyond the bounds of emphasized femininity; we require theory sensitive to how women/girls *as women/girls* occasionally commit violence.

A major result then of an exclusive concentration on male-female difference has been to either masculinize women/girls or direct theory away from issues that seriously complicate difference, such as race, age, and female engagement in "male crime." Feminists of color have, of course, berated much of social theory for assuming that all female experiences are similar. Scholars such as bell hooks (1984) have criticized the race bias that occurs when specific experiences of privileged white women are universalized as the experiences of all women. In the same way, criminological theory must not universalize female crime. Although second-wave feminism has disrupted assumptions about men and women and offered new ways to speak of "female crime," when girls and women engage in "male crime" it is as theoretically significant as when they engage in "female crime." Accordingly, such approaches as that suggested by Steffensmeier and Allan obscure a full and complete situational understanding of gender and crime: Where gender differences in crime are the exclusive focus, similarities in crime are often ignored or misrepresented. Abstracting gender from its social context and insensitive to issues of agency, such perspectives mask the possibility that gender patterns of crime may vary situationally, and that occasionally females and males engage in similar types and amounts of crime. As Karlene Faith (1993, p. 57) recently declared, to concentrate solely on crimes consistent with emphasized femininity "is to deny women's diversity and to promote gender-based objectification and stereotyping."

To comprehend the relation between masculinities and crime we must concurrently grasp when behavior normally thought to be masculine (i.e., interpersonal violence) is *not* a resource for constructing masculinity. As such, through an examination of "girls in the gang," I argue in Chapter 3 that the gang provides a milieu within which girls can experiment with, and possibly dismantle, the bounds of emphasized femininity. As they do this, however, are gang girls "doing masculinity?" I argue they are not. Partaking in the specific social situation of the gang, girls use the resources available to construct not masculinity but a specific type of femininity and, notwithstanding, challenge notions of gender as merely difference. Conceptualizing gender in terms of social situation and structured action permits a deeper formulation of not only what has been visible but what previously has been hidden or considered atypical "masculine" behavior, such as female violence. It also provides us with a more discerning portrait of masculinities, femininities, and crime.

Girls in the Gang

For both boys and girls, joining a youth gang represents an idealized collective solution to the lived experience of class and race power-lessness. For girls in particular, Karen Joe and Meda Chesney-Lind (1993, p. 10) point out that

> they exist in an environment that has little to offer young women of color. The possibility of a decent career, outside of "domestic servant," is practically nonexistent. Many come from distressed families held together by their mothers who are subsisting on welfare. Most have dropped out of school and have no marketable skills. Future aspirations are both gendered and unrealistic with the girls often expressing the desire to be rock stars or professional models when they are older.

In addition, alarmingly high rates of physical and sexual abuse have been reported for delinquent girls, ranging from a low of 40% to a high of 73% (Chesney-Lind & Shelden, 1992, p. 90; see also Campbell, 1993; Moore, 1991). In the social context of a bleak future and the overall violence that surrounds them in the street as well as at home, the youth gang becomes *family* to these girls. One Chicana ex-gang member (Moore, 1991, p. 77) reflects on how, for her, the gang

> was very important. Because that's all I had to look forward to, was my neighborhood, you know. That's all. It was my people—my neighborhood, my homies, my homeboys, my homegirls—that was everything to me. That was everything, you know. It wasn't all about my *familia*; it was all about my homeboys and homegirls.

Similarly, Harris (1988, p. 101) reported in her study of Latino gang girls that they exhibited a strong need for safety, belongingness, and companionship. One gang girl stated the importance of the gang in the following way: "It was family. We protected each other. We took care of each other. We stole for each other" (p. 119). And in a recent exploration into why girls join gangs in Hawaii, Joe and Chesney-Lind (1993, p. 20) argue that the gang "offers 'friendship' and a social support system for coping and managing their everyday life problems." One Samoan girl expressed it this way: "We all like sistas, all taking care of each other" (p. 21).

In short, the gang is where many lower working-class girls and boys of color develop strong "family" ties with members of their neighborhood—persons with whom they are not only acquainted but whom they perceive to be "like themselves." In the gang, a collective identity takes shape—they find companionship, safety, and a sense of belongingness (Fishman, 1988; Lauderback, Hansen, & Waldorf, 1992).

Street Culture and Gender Difference

Nevertheless, coming together on the street, girl-and-boy gang members interact to construct gender-separate groups; this appears to occur regardless of class and race position. Indeed, from the early works of Ashbury (1927) and Thrasher (1927), to the more recent research of Quicker (1983), Schwendinger and Schwendinger (1985), Harris (1988), Fishman (1988), Hagedorn (1988), Vigil (1988), and Moore (1991), young females have been found to construct "auxiliary" gangs to the male gangs. Notably, these auxiliary gangs are not simply composed of separate, identifiable groups but, rather, reflect gendered boundaries based on *power*. For example, Campbell's (1984/1991) important ethnographic study of lower working-class gangs in New York City reported that both females and males assume positions within the group that might be available to them in society at large. As Campbell (p. 266) points out, the "true gang" is composed of young males and specific female groups "exist as an annex to the male gang, [in which] the range of possibilities open to them is dictated and controlled by the boys." Similarly, Harris (1988, p. 128) reports that "while the girls purport to be independent of their male counterparts, belief in male superiority and the corresponding deference to male gang members became clear."

Other relevant research reports analogous gendered power relations in youth gangs and the construction of "girl gangs" as secondary to "male gangs" (Fishman, 1988; Moore, 1991). Thus, although girl gangs have limited autonomy, over their own rules and type of organization, they usually are connected yet subordinate to male gangs (Campbell, 1993, p. 132). Youth gangs, then, reflect the gender relations of power in society and the related discourse and practices by which they are reproduced. Consequently, gender difference here is in part related to the social construction of gendered dominance and subordination in gang arrangements.[1]

The realm of sexuality is also an important arena in gang life. Normative heterosexuality is a decisive "measuring rod" for group participation and a means by which gang members construct gendered difference. In the context of the gang, some sexual exploitation seems undeniable. For example, Schwendinger and Schwendinger (1985, p. 167) found that sexist exploitation of girls is common to both middle- and working-class youth groups. Similarly, a "homeboy" in Moore's (1991, p. 54) study stated: "I would say 90% was treated like a piece of ass. Usually we just used them as sexual need things, and companions. We needed companions in sex." Another male gang member from the same study echoed this position (p. 55):

> Ah, it's just there, you know what I mean. The—you know, when you want a *chapete* (fuck) it was there, you know what I mean. The guys treat them like shit, you know what I mean. And then when they want something you know, get it—wham bam. Sex. Just to have a partner for the time, you know. They were just there, you know, we used to get them in, throw a *linea* (lining up to have sex with a girl), you know what I mean.

Thus relationships of power and sexuality merge within the context of exploitation. Girl gang members are constructed as sexual objects, which concomitantly accentuates difference by emphasizing their "femaleness," and ultimately is an exercise of power over some girls' existence in the gang. Indeed, a female auxiliary gang that is defined primarily through its sexuality becomes a source of prestige and power among males in the gang.

Nevertheless, diversity exists in the way gangs construct heterosexual meanings. For example, Anne Campbell (1990, p. 179) found in New York girl gangs that "serial monogamy" was the norm and once a girl became involved with a boy she usually remained "faithful" until the relationship ended. These girls, then, construct a femininity that complies with emphasized femininity. Other research, however, indicates that doing difference through sexuality requires neither monogamy nor exploitation and, consequently, girls in gangs construct different types of femininity. For example, many girls effectively avert boys' claim to their bodies and actively negotiate the gang as a site for securing sexual pleasure (Carrington, 1993). As one gang girl stated to Joan Moore (1991, p. 55): "Not *me*, they didn't treat *me* like that. They think we're possessions, but we're not. No way. I pick my own boyfriends. I'll be with anybody I want to be with. You don't tell *me* who to be with." This girl has constructed an "opposition femininity" through sexuality; she has challenged culturally emphasized patterns. Alternatively, the Vice Queens "unabashedly placed themselves at the boys' disposal and openly encouraged them to fondle and have sexual relations with them" (Fishman, 1988, p. 17). Granting sexual favors to the Vice Kings was a means of gaining status among female peers in the gang, and thus is seen as a reinterpretation of emphasized femininity resulting in the construction of a unique type. Indeed, this type of femininity has its oppositional qualities as well; although the boys thought the girls were simply sexual objects of exploitation, status among the girls partially depended on "being able to keep four or five boys 'on the string' without any boys knowing of the others, but at the same time, avoiding sexual relationships with too many boys at one time" (p. 21).

For both boys and girls, then, the street gang is ideal for "doing gender" in terms of difference. By maintaining and emphasizing the "femaleness" of girl gang members, for example, through specific heterosexual meanings and practices, gender difference is preserved and specific types of masculinities and femininities are both validated and strengthened. Consequently, girl gang members are not simply passive recipients of "patriarchy," but actively participate in the construction of gender relations and they orchestrate the various forms of heterosexuality that result in varieties of femininity. Indeed, these girls do difference differently.

The gang, then, can be a site for sexual restriction and exploitation as well as for sexual exploration and pleasure and, thus, we find variety in terms of accommodation, reinterpretation, and opposition to emphasized femininity. Nevertheless, for the vast majority of girls, their significance in the gang is acquired through affiliation with boys. That is, gang girls accomplish gender in relation to the specific masculinities of the boys. This is so even for girls who develop the type of opposition femininity identified earlier.

Moreover, the street culture provides opposition to what gang girls see as the anachronistic and rigid values of their parents. For example, Campbell (1987, p. 456) describes Puerto Rican gang girls in New York who reject the "hicks" back on the island (Puerto Rico) and in contrast construct themselves as

> streetwise people who cannot be tricked, conned, or fooled. They know all the hustles and are not taken in by them. They strongly reject the old values and beliefs of the island, which they see as evidence of its backward status. . . . Gang members saw these beliefs and values as anachronistic and provincial.

Practices such as "coming home early" and "helping out with household chores" are seen as "old fashioned" in comparison to "hanging out on the street, dressing fashionably, flirting, getting 'high,' and attending parties" (Campbell, 1987, p. 454). Distancing themselves from, and therefore opposing, the provinciality of their race and class, gang girls are practicing a particularized race and class femininity. As agents in a unique historical, social, and situational setting, these girls negotiate a specific gender, race, and class identity and, in so doing, become something distinct from "Other."

Furthermore, members of youth gangs engage in "male" and "female" crimes as a resource for doing gender and satisfying the needs of the "fast life" on the street. For example, elsewhere (Messerschmidt, 1993, p. 108) I describe how, for male gang members, robbery is the most available criminal resource for obtaining money and constructing a specific type of masculinity: "Within the social setting of the street group, robbery is an acceptable practice for accomplishing gender"—and, therefore, doing difference. For girls, however, prostitution seems to be the principal criminal resource for obtaining "fast money" as well as doing difference.[2] A study of youth growing up poor in six different cities across the United States reported that in all of the cities "prostitution is the main occupation for girls" (Williams & Kornblum, 1985, p. 61). Moreover, Fishman (1988, p. 16) notes that all members of the Vice Queens participated in prostitution as their chief source of income:

> Customers were procured in taverns and on the street or at other locations not connected with organized houses of prostitution. The girls were aware of the prostituting activities of their peers and prostitution was accepted as standard behavior for the group.

Clearly, then, gender is a situated accomplishment in which individuals produce forms of behavior seen by others in the same immediate situation as either masculine or feminine. Within the confines and social settings of the street, economically marginal boys and girls form youth gangs partly to obtain "fast money" for adequate participation in street life. In similar fashion as "Detroit Red" discussed in Chapter 2, these youth participate in a street culture where work for "the man" is not the primary signifier of identity; rather, "fast money" is emphasized to pursue "the fast life." As Paul Gilroy (1990, p. 274) points out, the "hood" becomes the arena for celebrating the body as "an instrument of pleasure rather than an instrument of labor." The street is assertively and provocatively occupied by the pursuit of leisure and pleasure (p. 274). Here gender, race, and class are all salient; girl gang members situationally construct practices that counter their gender, race, and class subordinate position and such social action is the mechanism through which a specific race, class, and feminine identity take on meaning. "Hustling Johns" becomes a means of avoiding wage work and actively participating as a properly raced, classed, and gendered actor of street life. For example, girl gang members spend their "fast money" on food and shelter as well as the appropriate symbols of leisure/pleasure: drugs, alcohol, "trips to movies and steakhouses," and the "right" brand name of clothing and shoes (Campbell, 1987, p. 457). Indeed, as Campbell (pp. 457-458) found in her research, girls efforts to distance themselves from the "drabness" of their structured race and class position was also

> reflected in great concern about cleanliness in appearance. Although they sometimes referred to themselves as "out-laws," they never displayed the disregard for personal hygiene and appearance that has been described among biker groups like the Hells Angels. Getting ready to "hang out" often took some time because the girls were so meticulous about their clothing and make-up. Jeans were dry cleaned rather than washed, and boots were oiled and sneakers whitened every day.

Thus, their criminality incorporated dimensions and meanings of the street culture and, in turn, allowed them to display the appropriate "style" of that oppositional gender, race, and class culture.

Moreover, although the examples of robbery and prostitution show how some members of youth gangs produce "fast money" as well as race and class specific masculinities/femininities, it is through prostitution that these gang girls construct a femininity that both confirms and disaffirms emphasized femininity—yet simultaneously does difference. Prostitution confirms emphasized femininity in the sense that these girls construct themselves as sexually seductive to men and receptive to the sexual "drives" and special "needs" of men. In addition to these conventional aspects of femininity, however, involvement in prostitution also ridicules emphasized femininity by advocating extramarital sex, sex for pleasure, anonymous sex, and sex not limited to reproduction and the domesticated couple. This construction of a specific type of femininity, then, challenges and reinterprets emphasized femininity. The result is a gendered gang in which boys and girls do masculinity and femininity in a distinct race and class way—crime often used as a resource for facilitating the accomplishment of gender, race, and class difference.

Uniting for the "Hood"

In the daily life of the youth gang, girls not only participate in the social construction of difference but also engage in practices common to boys. Although there is a whole variety of common practices, most time is spent in such nondelinquent leisure activities as simply "hanging out" at a favorite spot or attending sporting and social events. In addition, boy and girl gang members partake in such delinquent activities as drinking, taking and selling drugs, committing theft, and fighting (Chesney-Lind & Shelden, 1992, p. 45; Lauderback et al., 1992).

The last activity, fighting, usually considered atypical gendered behavior by females, affords considerable insight into the diversity of gender construction. In fact, one recent feminist text identifies female violence as so rare that it is labeled as an "anomaly" and not in need of much further investigation (Faith, 1993, p. 100). From the point of view of privileged white women, female violence may indeed be infrequent and unusual, but for lower working-class girls of color in the United States, violence is far from an anomaly. Young lower working-class girls of color, in particular, African American girls, commit interpersonal crimes of violence at a much higher rate than do other girls. In a recent review of the literature, Sally Simpson (1991, pp. 117-118) reported that African American girls have higher rates of homicide and aggravated assault than white girls, and that girls of color participate in Uniform Crime Reports violent offenses 5.5 times as often as white girls (see also Sommers & Baskin, 1992). Moreover, violent crime rates are highest in lower-working-class communities—urban communities that are disproportionately racial minority in composition (Simpson, 1991, p. 119).

It is well established that the leading cause of death among African American male teenagers is homicide. Less well-known is the fact that homicide is the leading cause of death for African American women between the ages of 15 and 24 (U.S. Department of Health & Human Services, 1993, pp. 76-77). In addition, males are not always more likely than females to die by homicide. At every age until the late 40s, an African American female faces a higher risk of death by homicide than a white male (pp. 76-77).[3] Although the perpetrators of this homicide are overwhelmingly men,[4] a recent study (Mann, 1993, p. 219) of "sister against sister" homicide in six U.S. cities (with homicide rates equal to or higher than the national rate) found that women who kill other women basically resemble the portrait depicted over the past 2 decades by previous researchers: They are young, black, undereducated, and unemployed. Thus, they reflect the current American portrait of an expanding group of women of color who are marginal to the larger society.

This intragender violence by lower-working-class girls of color generally occurs within the context of the youth gang. Youth gangs confer a dubious prestige on *both* boys and girls with a proven ability to fight—boys and girls to whom street fighting is an essential source of meaning, reputation, and status. The development of this reputation begins during the initiation ceremony, for the gang will not accept just anyone. A female gang member (cited in Campbell, 1993, p. 136) describes one such initiation:

> We used to take a new girl to the park. Now that girl had to pick one of our girls. And whoever she wanted, she had to fight that girl to see that she could take the punches without crying. . . . Like if I'm walking down the street with you, you have to be able to count that I'm going to throw my life for you. Just like I expect you to do it for me. I have to be able to say, "I'm going to stay here and fight because I know you're going to stay here and fight too."

In East Los Angeles, girls become gang members by being "jumped in." One gang member explained the process to Quicker (1983, pp. 15-16):

Q: What happens when you get jumped in? What do they do?

R: When you get jumped in, what they do is they get around you and then there'll be a girl counting. Like there will be a girl out there and she'll go okay and then they'll start jumping you. She'll count to 10 and when she finishes counting, they'll stop.

Demonstration of toughness not only gains entrance to the gang but also proclaims oneself a "bad girl." Indeed, in girl gangs "the ability and willingness to fight, facing the enemy, not running from confrontation, to be 'bad,' to be 'crazy,' to be tough . . . are all prized behaviors" (Harris, 1988, p. 106). "Bad-girl" femininity serves to rank girls in terms of capacity to display physical violence and power;

girls who do not "measure up" are ignored and "jumped out" of the gang. Indeed, "bad girls" take pride in their fighting ability and their consequent acquired reputation and status. These girls accomplish gender by specific relational means that violently oppose other girls. Such social practice gains currency in relation to girls who fail to "qualify" and, predictably, constructs power relations among girls as the following comment (Campbell, 1987, pp. 462-463) indicates:

> Girls around here see a girl that's quiet, they think that she's a dud. Yeah— let's put it that way. They think they don't know how to fight. . . . Round here you have to know how to fight. I'm glad I got a reputation. That way nobody will start with me—they *know*, you know. They're going to come out losing. Like all of us, we got a reputation. We're crazy. Nobody wants to fight us for that reason —you know. They say "No, man. That girl might stab me or cut my face or something like that."

Differences among girls hinge on how they construct femininity. Thus, "bad-girl" femininity is sustained through its relation to situationally defined "dud" femininity, even within similar race and class categories. Gang girls are distinguished from nongang girls through different constructions of femininity. Lower-working-class African American girls share the experience of race and class oppression but the notions of "bad girl" and "dud" inflects their commonality with difference. This represents what Friedman (1995, p. 30) identifies as a partial and situational displacement of the White/Other binary: "The category of Other explodes into its heterogeneous parts while the category of whiteness remains fixed and monolithic." Thus, as agents living out their race and class subordinate position, girls construct power/powerlessness in relation to each other.

Similarly, in gangs that emphasize heterosexual monogamy for girls but not for boys (because it is considered "unnatural" for boys to refuse offers of sex), girl violators are controlled fiercely, as the following example (Campbell, 1984/1991, p. 258) shows:

> "Hey, I hear you made it with my old man." This and that. And blat, and that's it. The whole thing is over 'cus they don't even raise their hands. They put their head down and they cut out fast. 'Cus

they know—like if I was hitting a girl and they hit me back and all *these* girls see it, they're all gonna get in, you know? And she's going to get a worse beating. So she takes a slap or two and goes home and cries.

In this situation, not only is a specific type of heterosexuality reproduced, but power relations between girls and femininities are constructed—monogamy is privileged and enhanced through violent attack (and group support for that attack) on situationally constituted promiscuity.

Probably the most positively sanctioned site for displaying one's "badness" is participating in *group* violence. Bonding with peers of common residence, marginalized youths tend to develop a collective race and class loyalty to their neighborhood and to form territorial control over their turf or "hood" (Messerschmidt, 1993). The street is inculcated with a powerful sense of locality and a street gang's specific territory, carefully branded and defended at levels of conspicuous absurdity, defines the gang and its perimeters of activity. The focus here is to defend and extend gang space for independence from "the system" and, thus, create a place for self-rule. In fact, turf serves as a boundary between groups and as an arena of status and potential conflict. The "territoriality of identity" becomes simultaneously the "territoriality of control" (Gilroy, 1990, p. 278) and, therefore, street gangs are intolerant of invasions of their space by outsiders. When outsiders do invade their local "hood," this is viewed as inherently offensive. One gang member explains how easily a fight erupts when entering another girl-gang's turf (Harris, 1988, p. 104):

> Like if you go somewhere. Let's suppose we go to San Fernando. And like we don't get along with San Fernando. And like we go to the park and a bunch of girls from SanFer are over there, and us Blythe Street Girls. And they're going to give us hard looks, and we're going to give them hard looks, and that's where it's going to start. And they'll say, "Where are you from?"
>
> "Blythe Street. Where are you from?"
>
> "Well, fuck you." And then we go. Just for the street. Uno Blythe. Blythe Street's number one. That's all it is.

As the quoted scenario indicates, it is not the territory per se that is significant, but the local group's identification with that particular territory. Indeed, support for the group (as representative of the neighborhood) is held in highest esteem and fighting exhibits loyalty to the "hood" and, therefore, to the gang (Fishman, 1988, p. 14). If a gang girl cannot or will not fight, she is summarily rejected. As one gang girl explained to Harris (1988, p. 109):

> You can belong as long as you can back up your shit and don't rat on your homegirls or back away. If you don't back them up and you run, we'll jump that girl out because she ain't going to take care of nothing. All she wants is our backup and our support but she ain't going to give us none of hers, so what's the use of her being around! She has to be able to hold up the hood.

Clearly, one shores up the hood through violence. As Harris (1988, p. 174) goes on, girls in gangs "will fight instead of flee, assault instead of articulate, and kill rather than control their aggression." Indeed, for "girls in the gang," status is not achieved from excellence in school or at work but, rather, through "the perfection of fighting techniques" and "the number of times the girls willingly fought and with whom they fought" (Fishman, 1988, p. 23). Thus, in relation to middle-class white people, gang girls are lower-working-class girls of color, but in relation to each other they are set apart according to constituency in a particular "hood."

In the world of the street, different gangs are allocated different "hoods" and those who venture out of their socially defined neighborhood are chastised and punished. In this social situation, boys and girls unite on the basis of neighborhood. Because gender is not static but dynamic, in a race and class specific social context where "hood" is elevated to preeminence (that is, neighborhood differences become highly salient) the path for similarity in behavior is much less obstructed. In the context of the street fight, interaction involves at once *caring* (for the "hood" and other gang members) and also *physically aggressive* practices (against another gang) by *both* boys and girls. Moreover, the criteria of femininity are embedded in specific social situations and recurrent practices within them. In the particular context of the youth gang, the criteria of "bad-girl" femininity involve physical strength and power as resources for publicly demonstrating individual proficiency at defending the "hood" by conquering adversary gang girls. Indeed, girls (as representatives of a rival "hood") are the subject of competition in the struggle to secure a situationally specific feminine identity. In other words, what is usually considered atypical feminine behavior outside this situation is, in fact, *normalized* within the social context of interneighborhood conflict; girl-gang violence in this situation is encouraged, permitted, and privileged by *both* boys and girls as appropriate feminine behavior. Thus, "bad-girl" femininity is situationally accomplished and context-bound within the domain of the street.

Girl-gang violence, however, is sometimes subordinated to boy-gang violence. For example, in some gangs girls serve merely as weapon carriers for the boys and, if needed, as "backups" (Chesney-Lind & Shelden, 1992, pp. 45-46). As one gang girl expressed to Harris (1988, p. 127):

> Yah, we back up the homeboys. . . . And if they were into a fight, somehow it will get to us and we will go and back them up, even though we're girls and we're from the Tiny Locas, we'll still back up our homeboys.

Thus, girl-gang violence in this setting occurs within the context of gender relations of power; these girls are doing femininity in a specific way through their affiliation and, therefore, relation to boys. In other words, they are accommodating to masculine dominance.

Girl-gang violence is not always marginal and secondary, however, to boy-gang violence. For example, with regard to her gang's involvement in violence, one gang girl stated (Harris, 1988, p. 127): "We would do our thing and they would do their thing." In other words, girls are involved routinely in violence without the boys being present. Even when boys are nearby, the boys may actually play a secondary role as "backups" (pp. 127-128):

> The guys would back us up sometimes. They'll be there. And they'll watch out like two girls on one or something and they'll get one

girl off. Whenever they seen that one of us was getting more hurt. But it usually didn't happen that way. We usually didn't need backup that much. . . . But they'll be there because sometimes guys came from other gangs and they want to get on the girls too, so like they'll be there in case the other guys came.

For girls in the gang, doing femininity means occasionally, and in appropriate circumstances, doing violence. Because participation in violence varies depending on the setting, girls are, however, assessed and held accountable as "bad-girls" differently. Given that gang girls realize their behavior is accountable to other girls and boys in the gang, they construct their actions in relation to how those actions will be interpreted by others in the same social context. These girls, then, are doing femininity, race, and class in terms of activities appropriate to their sex, race, and class category in specific social situations.

Accordingly, violence by young women in youth gangs should not be interpreted as an attempt to be "male" and "pass" as the other gender. Yet, in the past as well as today some women do pass successfully as men, in part to acquire male privileges.[5] For example, a study of "gender-blending females," young women who pass as men in public settings, found that these women were better treated and were generally afforded more respect in public as "men" than they were in public as women. As Devor (1987, p. 34) concludes, these women passed as men to obtain greater privileges and freedom of movement while simultaneously avoiding some of "the odious aspects of being female in a society predicated on male dominance."

Arguably, then, girls in youth gangs are not attempting to pass as boys or as "gender-blending females" in the previously mentioned sense. Indeed, these girls value emphasized femininity, for the most part display themselves as feminine in culturally "appropriate" ways, and do not construct an ambiguous gender outside the gang milieu. As Campbell (1993, p. 133) points out, gang girl concern

with their appearance, their pride in their ability to attract men, their sense of responsibility as mothers left me in no doubt that they enjoyed being women. They didn't want to be like men and, indeed, would have been outraged at such a suggestion.

Girl-gang violence is but one practice in the overall process of constructing a specific type of femininity, race, and class. Accordingly, femininity is assessed both in terms of willingness to defend the "hood" and on doing difference. Thus, within the gang, girl members do most of, if not all, the cooking and child care, prepare the food and drink for "partying," and are "very fussy" over gender display (clothes, hair, makeup) (Campbell, 1984/1991; Vigil, 1988, pp. 111-112). By engaging in such practices girl-gang members are not simply preparing, for example, the necessities for adequate "partying"—they also are producing gender difference. As West and Zimmerman (1987, p. 144) point out, for women to engage in this type of labor and men not to engage in it represents for both an opportunity for doing difference. In addition to carrying out the practices of doing difference identified earlier—separate but connected gendered gangs, specific forms of heterosexuality, and "gender-appropriate" crimes—by engaging in activities identified with emphasized femininity, girl-gang members are assessed successfully as women, even when participating actively in street violence. Accordingly, their "bad-girl" femininity consists of a combination of conventional gender practices (such as cooking and child care) and atypical gender practices (such as violence)—each practice justified by appropriate circumstances. Thus, the case of gang girls exhibits a unique fluidity of gender in which different gender identities are emphasized or avoided depending on the social setting. Indeed, within the social context of the gang, "bad-girls" construct a femininity that secures approval as members of the gang and as women.

This fluctuating femininity bears a striking resemblance to the femininity constructed by women in the U.S. Marines. As the following quote indicates, certain events demand "hard" femininity while others justify emphasized femininity, paralleling the flexibility of gender accomplishment seen among girls in youth gangs (Williams, 1989, p. 76):

> Like when we're marching, the woman part drops out. It's just recruits out marching, slamming our heels down on the deck. When we're not in our cammies or out marching, it's put on your makeup and say yes or no, and don't bend down with your knees apart.

Similarly to "bad-girls," these women are constructing a femininity that wins acceptance as "marines" and as women.

Moreover, Barrie Thorne (1993) recently reported in her important work on gender in elementary schools that when classroom events are organized around an absorbing task, such as a group art project, the cooperation encouraged between boys and girls helps to clear a path toward gender similarity. Likewise, for both boys and girls in the gang, one of the most absorbing tasks is common defense of the "hood." Indeed, the symbolic essence of the gang is triggered and becomes meaningful only through interneighborhood conflict. In this social situation, gang boys and girls unite and work together to protect "their neighborhood" from the threat of adjacent neighborhood gangs. As Campbell (1987, p. 459) points out, girl-gang members see themselves as part of "a vigilante force on behalf not only of themselves but of friends and neighbors too." Under such conditions *gender* difference becomes secondary to *group* difference and the result is a social site for the construction of "bad-girl" femininity.

Conclusion

Owing to their position in gender, race, and class divisions of labor and power, many young, marginalized girls of color form or join violent street gangs. They adapt to economic and racial powerlessness by competing with rivals of their own gender, race, and class to protect their "hood." For girls in the gang, the struggle with other young women of their class (and usually race) is a means for constructing a specific race and class femininity. As Anne Campbell (1987, pp. 463-464) would put it, these girls are African American, Chicana, or Puerto Rican, but not provincial; they are lower-working-class but not drab; they celebrate emphasized femininity but are not passive. Because girls in the gang collectively experience their everyday world from a specific position in society, they construct femininity in a uniquely race and class appropriate way.

The girls-in-the-gang illustration reveals how social structures are constituted by social action and, in turn, provide resources for doing race, class, and femininity in particularized ways. As resources for doing gender, race, and class, the distinct types of youth crime ultimately are based on these social structures. In this way social structures both constrain and enable social action and, therefore, gender, race, class and youth crime.

Gender patterns of crime are not static, but vary situationally. Outside parental and school surveillance, the gang provides greater space for the negotiation of gender, race, and class. Consequently, females and males engage in "gender-appropriate" crimes yet sometimes commit similar types of crimes. By developing a sense of gender, race, and class as structured action and situational accomplishment, we isolate not only the social actions that sustain but also those that undermine the construction of gender, race, class, and crime as difference.

The gang provides a milieu within which girls can experiment with, and possibly dismantle, the bounds of emphasized femininity. Girl gang members use the race and class resources available to construct gender and, in so doing, challenge notions of gender as merely difference. Thus, rather than conceptualizing gendered crime simplistically in terms of, for example, "males commit violence and females commit theft," we are now able to explore which males and which females commit which crimes, and in which social situations.

Notes

1. Not all female gangs are connected to male gangs. Independent girl gangs do exist but seem to be rare. A recent notable example of such a gang is the "Potrero Hill Posse" in San Francisco (see Lauderback et al., 1992).

2. Other primary money-making activities by girl gangs are drug dealing and shoplifting (for an example, see Lauderback et al., 1992).

3. This is *not* to suggest, as is regularly portrayed in the mass media, the emergence of a "new violent female criminal." On the contrary, I agree with Meda Chesney-Lind (1993, p. 339) who recently documented that "girls have long been members of gangs, that their roles in these gangs have been considerably more varied than early stereotypes would have it, and that girls' occasionally violent behavior has, during other decades, been largely ignored."

4. This raises an important issue that has been ignored in the criminological and feminist literature—intragang cross-gender violence as a form of "family violence."

5. For example, in the 1850s, one

Lucy Ann Lobdell left her husband in upstate New York and passed as a man to support herself. "I made up my mind to dress in men's attire to seek labor," she explained, and to earn "men's wages." Later, she became the Reverend Joseph Lobdell and set up house with Maria Perry, living for 10 years as man and wife. (D'Emilio & Freedman, 1988, pp. 124-125)

Similarly, in another case in mid-1800s New York,

a woman took the name Murray Hall and began to dress as a man. She opened an employment bureau, settled down with the first of her two wives, and later adopted a daughter. Hall became influential in the Tammany Hall Democratic political machine and earned a reputation for drinking, playing poker, and being "sweet on women." (D'Emilio & Freedman, 1988, p. 125)

Chapter **4**

Murderous Managers

It has been over 10 years since the space shuttle *Challenger* exploded in midair, just 73 seconds into flight, killing all seven crew members. The President's Commission (1986) investigating the explosion concluded that the loss of *Challenger* was due to a failure in the joint between two segments of the right solid rocket booster (SRB). O-rings, intended to prevent hot gases from escaping through the joint during the propellant burn of the rocket engine, failed to seal properly because of the extremely cold temperature at launch time (29 degrees F). More specifically, the cold temperature impaired O-ring resiliency, allowing the hot gases to escape, ignite, and within seconds penetrate the external tank.[1]

The President's Commission (1986) further concluded that problems with the O-ring design were well documented, and therefore well-known, by both government (NASA) and corporate (Morton Thiokol, Inc.) officials years before that fateful day. Indeed, the Commission concluded that the explosion was "rooted in history" and that a "flawed decision-making process" led to the launch (President's Commission, 1986, p. 82).

In addition to the President's Commission, criminological investigations of the explosion have appeared in recent years, focusing primarily on the organizational context within which the "flawed decision" to launch was reached (Kramer, 1992; Vaughan, 1989, 1994, 1996). This chapter contributes to this evolving reexamination of the explosion by considering the fact, which previous investigations ignore, that those involved in the decision to launch *Challenger* were all men; my interest is the gendered (and class) character of the events and decisions leading to the *Challenger* explosion. Indeed, such an investigation opens a window to corporate decision making, generating new insights into hegemonic masculinities and corporate crime.[2]

Moreover, this chapter adds to our ongoing exploration of how and in what respects masculinity is constituted in certain settings at certain times, and how that construct relates to crime. For example, as discussed in the Prologue, work in the paid labor market is central to hegemonic masculinity and, therefore, to the lives of most men. Indeed, "the job" is a major basis of identity and what it means to be a man. For criminology, however, the association among masculinity, work, and crime historically has been explored only in the case of *unemployed* men engaged in street crime. And routinely at issue here is not the unemployed male's relationship to work per se but, rather, his limited or lack of access to the paid labor market. What is missing in the criminological and gender studies literature is a full consideration of gender and crime within the context of work and, especially, in the setting of white-collar work. This chapter attempts to fill that void by examining the relationship between masculinity, class, and crime involving white male managers and engineers in a particular corporate organizational setting.

The focus of the remaining sections, then, explores the differentiation of hegemonic masculinities by observing the work and product of their construction in a specific setting and through certain practices. I examine such masculinities not in terms of relations between women and men, but as they are reproduced among men in corporations. A review of the empirical evidence on the space shuttle *Challenger* explosion, with an eye to the social context in which both gender and corporate crime are accomplished, reveals that gender is a critical structural tool in corporations. Indeed, the definition and interpretation of the boundaries between masculinities, and thus the hierarchical separation of some men from other men, are critical organizational bases in corporate bureaucracies. Accordingly, the specific masculine meanings constructed through particular occupations and the ways in which corporate crime is related to those meanings and occupations must be analyzed thoroughly. As such, I argue that only through an analysis of hegemonic masculinities can we make coherent sense of the space shuttle *Challenger* explosion. The space shuttle *Challenger* explosion provides an excellent case study of how in the same social situation, one type of hegemonic masculinity (manager) was constructed through the commission of corporate crime while contemporaneously another type of hegemonic masculinity (engineer) was constructed through resisting that crime.

Risky Technology

The National Aeronautics and Space Administration (NASA) had long been interested in frequent, economical access to space and, in 1970, the White House declared that funding on the order of previous NASA projects, such as *Gemini* and *Apollo*, was no longer possible (President's Commission, 1986, p. 2). Thus, to obtain funding from Congress, NASA had to guarantee a program with low development costs and dependable routine operations. To accomplish this, NASA proposed a space shuttle that would be both reusable and cost-effective in design.[3] Moreover, the shuttle was to be economically self-sufficient through satellite launchings and commercially supported in-flight research. It was in the increasingly austere fiscal environment of the early 1970s then that the shuttle was born (p. 4).

Morton Thiokol, Inc. (MTI) was selected on November 20, 1973 to receive the NASA contract to design and build the SRBs. Not surprisingly, costs were the primary concern of NASA's selection board.[4] Although the board noted several problems with the MTI proposal, they were deemed "technical in nature" and "the costs to correct did not negate the MTI cost advantage." Furthermore, the dual O-ring feature was especially noteworthy to the selection board.[5] Thus, a cost-plus-award-fee contract, worth approximately $800 million, was awarded to MTI (President's Commission, 1986, p. 121).

From the beginning, however, there were problems with MTI's dual O-ring design, all of which were well documented by both NASA and MTI.[6] Despite consistent evidence of the hazardous nature of the O-ring design, shuttle missions were not halted to correct the anomalies. In fact, as the President's Commission (p. 5) points out, with the landing of the fourth test flight, "the orbital flight test program came to an end [and remarkably] NASA declared the space shuttle 'operational.' " Initially, managers and engineers at both NASA's Marshall Space Flight Center in Huntsville, Alabama (which has authoritative responsibility for the orbiter's main engine, the external tank, and the solid rocket booster) and at MTI incessantly rationalized that after some initial erosion, the O-rings would ultimately seal intact; if the primary O-ring failed to seal the joint, the secondary O-ring would act as a back-up. Flight after flight was approved by both organizational managers and engineers, "accepting the possibility of some O-ring erosion due to hot gas impingement" and the belief that redundancy would prevail (p. 132).[7]

By January 24, 1985, however, when the 15th shuttle flight was launched, the temperature of the O-rings at launch was 53 degrees F, the coldest launch temperature to that date. On that flight, O-ring erosion occurred in both SRBs as well as in both primary and secondary O-rings. Accordingly, several MTI *engineers* became much more concerned and reported to Marshall that this launch occurred during the "worst-case temperature change in Florida history" and that "low temperature enhanced the probability of erosion" (President's Commission, 1986, p. 136). Although previously MTI engineers felt the possibility existed for significant reduction of the erosion problem and a belief in redundancy, the results of this flight clearly indicated the anomalies needed to be corrected immediately. As Roger Boisjoly (1987, p. 4), the leading engineering specialist at MTI, stated in a letter to MTI management:

> This letter is written to ensure that management is fully aware of the seriousness of the current O-ring erosion problem in the SRB joints from an engineering standpoint. . . . It is my honest and very real fear that if we do not take immediate action to dedicate a team to solve the problem, with the field joint having the number one priority, then we stand in jeopardy of losing a flight along with all the launch pad facilities.[8]

MTI management was not, however, forthcoming with the resources necessary to solve the O-ring problem. As Boisjoly (1987, p. 1) goes on to point out: "the MTI management style would not let anything compete or interfere with the production and shipping of boosters."

Thus, by 1985, the O-ring erosion problem had been well documented at Marshall and MTI, yet the management of both organizations ignored engineer concerns and labeled the problem an "acceptable risk" rather than suspending shuttle missions until the problem was fixed. In addition, in that same year NASA published a projection calling for 24 flights per year by 1990.

Arguably, NASA was under pressure throughout the early- to mid-1980s to meet both customer commitments and Congressional approval —which meant not only launch a certain number of flights per year but launch them on time. Indeed, as the President's Commission (1986, p. 164) concludes:

> From the inception of the shuttle, NASA had been advertising a vehicle that would make space operations "routine and economical." The greater the annual number of flights, the greater the degree

of routinization and economy, so heavy emphasis was placed on the schedule.

Within this context, Marshall managers responded to the O-ring problem not by canceling flights and fixing the problem (because delays were to be avoided), but by proceeding full speed ahead. As the President's Commission (1986, p. 152) put it, in the face of "unrelenting pressure to meet the demands of an accelerating flight schedule," these managers considered the faulty seal "nonserious" and an "acceptable risk." The result was a pattern of risk-taking practices by Marshall managers.

Whereas Marshall managers faced the imperative of a routine and economical flight schedule, MTI faced far-reaching contract negotiations with NASA and competition from other aerospace suppliers and manufacturers. As Malcolm McConnell (1987, pp. 180-181) argues, negotiations between NASA and MTI regarding the second phase of the lucrative shuttle SRB contract were intensely troubling for MTI throughout much of 1985:

> In the 1970s contract, Thiokol was assigned the production of the first 37 sets of boosters. Given the increased flight schedule, that number would be used by the end of 1986. Therefore, Thiokol was actively negotiating for the second-phase contract that would cover the next 60 sets of boosters, a procurement award worth a billion dollars. However, other aerospace companies had been lobbying Congress for at least 2 years to force NASA to break Morton Thiokol's monopoly on producing the SRB's. In the fall of 1985 Thiokol's management was acutely aware of this lobbying effort, which Congressional staff members called a "full-court press," by Thiokol's competitors.

Indeed, by winter of 1985 NASA initiated competitive bidding on the pending contract renewal, "thus seriously threatening for the first time Thiokol's 13-year monopoly" (McConnell, 1987, p. 60). Consequently, MTI managers were not in the position to irritate their most prominent customer by suspending shuttle flights until a new O-ring design was developed. So they, in the manner of their counterparts at Marshall, accepted escalating risk. In short, both Marshall and MTI management came to accept the O-ring problem as an "unavoidable and an acceptable flight risk" (President's Commission, 1986, p. 148).

The Launch Decision

On January 27, 1986, NASA scrubbed the scheduled flight due to high crosswinds at the launch site and rescheduled *Challenger* for the following morning (President's Commission, 1986, p. 17). By the early afternoon of January 27, 1986, MTI engineers became increasingly concerned over the predicted low temperature of 29 degrees F for the rescheduled launch time, especially in light of the near disaster one year earlier at 53 degrees F. This concern led ultimately to a teleconference between Marshall and MTI officials on the issue of temperature. Data regarding the effect of low temperature on the O-rings and the joint seal were presented by MTI engineers along with an opinion that launch should be delayed until the temperature was at least 53 degrees F. Marshall requested that MTI prepare and telefax a more formal presentation to both Marshall and Kennedy Space Center officials (in Florida) for a full-fledged teleconference later that evening (President's Commission, 1986, p. 106).

At approximately 8:45 p.m. EST, the second teleconference commenced. The telefax presented a history of the O-ring erosion in the SRB joints of previous flights. Roger Boisjoly, the leading engineering specialist at MTI, expressed deep concern about launching at such low temperature (President's Commission, 1986, p. 88). Boisjoly argued that the Shuttle should not be launched below a temperature of 53 degrees F because such temperature would result in the O-rings becoming less resilient and, therefore, incapable of sealing the joint before hot gases ignited to cause an explosion. As Boisjoly stated to the President's Commission (p. 89), it would be "like trying to shove a brick into a crack versus a sponge." Indeed, by now both MTI management and engineers agreed that the shuttle should not launch until temperatures reached at least 53 degrees F. Notwithstanding, Marshall managers "were not pleased" with MTI's conclusions and recommendations (p. 90).

Marshall challenged MTI's data and conclusions primarily by accusing MTI of trying to establish new launch-commit criteria based on a 53-degree F standard. Eventually, Lawrence Mulloy, SRB manager at Kennedy, responded to MTI's concern about temperature by stating: "My God, Thiokol, when do you want me to launch, next April?" (President's Commission, 1986, p. 96). Mulloy (p. 1529) insisted that MTI's position was irrationally qualitative, based simply on experience rather than rational, quantifiable, evidence. A further exchange between MTI and NASA representatives continued for quite some time, MTI maintaining that launch should not occur outside the 53-degree F database. George Hardy, deputy director of science and engineering at Marshall, responded by stating: "I'm appalled at your recommendation" (p. 94).

Thus, MTI found themselves on the defensive and experienced formidable coaxing to reverse their no-launch recommendation. MTI was placed in a social situation where they had to demonstrate convincingly it was *not* safe to launch, whereas in all previous preflight conferences MTI was required to verify it was safe to launch. In other words, they had to prove the launch would fail![9]

Eventually the debate reached impasse. Overwhelmed at having to prove that the joint would fail, MTI management sought a 5-minute off-line recess to reevaluate the effect of temperature on the O-rings (President's Commission, 1986, p. 92). The caucus (lasting at least 30 minutes) began with Jerry Mason, senior vice president at MTI, stating to the three managers around him, "we have to make a management decision" (p. 92). Assuming that management was about to consider reversing the earlier no-launch decision, the MTI engineers (especially Roger Boisjoly and Arnie Thompson) attempted a last-minute explanation of the effects of low temperature on O-ring resiliency. Boisjoly explained this attempt to the President's Commission (pp. 92-93):

> Arnie actually got up from his position, which was down the table, and walked up the table and put a quarter pad down in front of the management folks, and tried to sketch out once again what his concern was with the joint, and when he realized he wasn't getting through, he just stopped.

> I tried one more time with the photos. I grabbed the photos, and I went up and discussed the photos once again and tried to make the point that it was my opinion from actual observations that temperature was indeed a discriminator and we should not ignore the physical evidence that we had observed. . . . I also stopped when it was apparent that I couldn't get anybody to listen.

In short, these two engineers ardently tried to stop management from reversing their earlier unanimous no-launch decision.

During this exchange, it was clear that three of the four managers supported a launch, but that Bob Lund, vice president of engineering, remained committed to the earlier no-launch decision (President's Commission, 1986, p. 108). After some further discussion of the data, with Lund remaining the sole holdout among the managers, Mason turned to Lund and instructed him "to take off his engineering hat and put on his management hat" (p. 93). The managers then agreed they had to make a management decision, as Mason states, "to conclude what we needed to conclude" (p. 1383). At this point the engineers were excluded from the decision-making process and a final management review was conducted by the four managers only. The MTI managers, then, with Lund concurring, decided to reverse the decision of the engineers and approve the launch for the next morning. As the President's Commission (p. 96) put it:

> At approximately 11 p.m. EST, the Thiokol/NASA teleconference resumed, the Thiokol management stating that they had reassessed the problem, that the temperature effects were a concern, but that the data were admittedly inconclusive. Kilminster read the rationale recommending launch and stated that that was Morton Thiokol's recommendation.

Managing to Kill

How can we begin to understand the fact that, in the face of a strong possibility of risk to human life, MTI engineers recognized this threat and argued against the launch whereas MTI managers yielded to pressure from Marshall and voted unanimously to launch?[10] It is now well established in the sociological literature that gender is embedded in corporations and that gender is accomplished through concrete corporate activities, resulting not only in gender divisions (e.g., gender divisions of labor; "male" and "female" jobs) but, also, in situationally specific gendered images, symbols, and practices (Acker, 1992). More specifically, corporations often are defined through metaphors of masculinity. Joan Acker (p. 253) states the following:

> Today, organizations are lean, mean, aggressive, goal oriented, efficient, and competitive but rarely empathetic, supportive, kind, and caring. Organizational participants actively create these images in their efforts to construct organizational cultures that contribute to competitive success.

The gendering of corporations involves a presentation of self as a gendered member of the corporation and, for the corporate manager, this means specific practices, such as rationality, instru- mentalism, careerism, decisiveness, productivism, and risk taking, that help the corporation be successful (Kerfoot & Knights, 1993, p. 671). Indeed, as we have known for almost 20 years, corporate- managerial masculinity is measured by success in reaching corporate goals; accordingly, managerial gendered practices align themselves with corporate needs (Acker, 1990; Kanter, 1977; Tolson, 1977).

MTI managers, like other corporate managers, pursued such gendered practices to assist MTI in attaining its goals. Like other corporate managers, MTI managers consistently faced economic pressures that focus on the present and the near future: "the *next* milestone, the *next* contract, and the *next* stockholders' report are 'real' near-terms subjects that a manager must always address" (Dubinskas, 1988, p. 195). As indicated, the immediate situational goal of MTI was to preserve a lucrative government contract. Given the social situation of uncertainty in reaching this goal caused by the O-ring problem, rather than "hang tough" and continue to oppose the launch, MTI management engaged in risk-taking behavior to achieve their corporate objective. MTI managers rationalized giving greater weight to the advantage of risk-taking practices over halting shuttle flights until the O-ring problem could be fixed. They chose the risk-taking path as more likely to advance both their individual masculine performance (gender) as well as corporate success (social class). Although all major MTI managerial decision makers were "white," the social construction of a specific type of "whiteness" was not the salient feature to this situation as were gender and class. In other words, gender and class were directly threatened (and, thus, accountability) by the O-ring problem but not race.

When managers talk about "what is at stake" in their jobs, the answer invariably is "the growth of the organization" and, hence, their ultimate status (Dubinskas, 1988, p. 199). Interviews with corporate managers show that they regard a manager who fails to take risks as one who should not be in the business of managing, and risk taking is especially warranted when faced with possible failure to meet corporate goals (March & Shapira, 1987, pp. 1408-1409). To be sure, for managers faced with such uncertainty in meeting goals, "the desire to reach the target focuses attention in a way that leads generally to risk taking. In this case, the opportunities for gain receive attention, rather than the dangers" (March & Shapira, 1987, p. 1413). Thus, we should not be surprised that the MTI managers reversed the decision of the engineers and approved the launch. Indeed, prestige accompanies the advocacy of such risk taking and advocates of risk are perceived as especially capable managers, particularly when successful on the previous occasion (p. 1414).[11]

In this context, then, for MTI managers risk taking became the situational defining feature of managerial masculinity. Risk taking is widely documented as a masculine practice, where risk-laden social situations are responded to more often by men/boys than women/girls as a challenge, an opportunity to "prove" one's worth and demonstrate prowess to others (Arch, 1993, p. 4).[12] The MTI managers were no different from many other men confronted with a risk-laden situation; doing risk taking for them was, simultaneously, doing masculinity. What is different is that this risk-taking masculine practice was specific to the particular class standing of the managers and the social situation of this corporation. Clearly, the unique social conditions surrounding *Challenger* flights, preserving a lucrative government contract, created a context for MTI managers to push the

limits of SRB technology. Because these managers had to demonstrate
that the SRBs could survive a rigorous flight schedule, rather than
acknowledge design flaws they demonstrated corporate-managerial
competence by supporting the necessity for remaining on schedule.
Thus risk taking became an available resource for achieving corporate
goals because they "got away with it last time." As one member of the
President's Commission (1986, p. 148) observed:

> [The shuttle] flies [with O-ring erosion] and nothing happens. Then
> it is suggested, therefore, that the risk is no longer so high for the
> next flights. We can lower our standards a little bit because we got
> away with it last time.

In other words, because flight after flight was "successful" (an
explosion did not occur), this rationalized further risk taking. Having
survived the challenge, MTI managers became increasingly comfort-
able continuing the risk-taking behavior; thus, risk taking became a
practice not only for securing corporate goals but for solving the
gender and class accountability problem at "the job." Doing risk
taking was not solely a practice for demonstrating corporate loyalty,
but simultaneously for rendering such action accountable in terms of
the normative conceptions and activities appropriate to the male sex
and class categories in this corporation. Because threats to profit-
making are concurrent threats to corporate-manager masculine accomplishment, risk taking is an acceptable means of resolving both
problems: risk taking is a resource in this particular setting for
accomplishing profit (class) and masculinity (gender) and, therefore,
merge into one entity. That is, MTI managers conflate a masculine
practices with profit-making practices. Accordingly, risk taking was
normalized among MTI management, permitting these men to draw
on previously formed risk-taking behavior as a resource for doing a
specific type of hegemonic masculinity. In short, managerial risk
taking became an institutionalized practice, a masculine resolution to
the spectacle of technological uncertainty.

Thus, MTI managers gave Marshall the green light to launch in
order to, as the President's Commission (1986, p. 104) stated: "ac-
commodate a major customer." Indeed, throughout "the first 3 weeks

of January 1986, NASA and Thiokol conducted negotiations over a $1 billion dollar contract," and extremely important contract discussions were scheduled for January 28th, "the day after Thiokol managers made their recommendation to proceed with the launch, the day the *Challenger* was destroyed" (McConnell, 1987, p. 60). Given this milieu, agreeing to take the risk demonstrated not only loyalty to the corporation but, simultaneously, provided MTI managers with a resource for doing masculinity, and, simultaneously, corporate crime, in that specific social setting.

Moreover, the attraction to risk taking by these corporate managers had as much to do with the social action itself as with what it produced in terms of corporate goals. The validation of manager effectiveness at MTI was one's proclivity to "go to the limit" in bringing a flight to "successful" fruition (President's Commission, 1986, p. 110). Each victorious challenge reconfirmed for others one's identity as an accomplished, proficient manager. Fervently effectuating risk-taking social practices provided these managers with the opportunity to exercise diligent control over the situation and bring it to a triumphant conclusion. This is consistent with other research on corporate-manager masculinity, which indicates that such managers are ranked "in terms of their capacity to display attributes of control over the definition of the reality of events" and are "constantly preoccupied with purposive action in the drive to be 'in control' " (Kerfoot & Knights, 1993, pp. 671-672). Thus, every successful launch was taken as proof that one was "in control" and, therefore, possessed "the right stuff" to be a *man*(ager).[13] Indeed, the "enterprise of winning" by overcoming danger is for managers "life consuming" and results in "an inward turned competitiveness, focused on the self, creating, in fact, an instrumentality of the personal" (Donaldson, 1993, p. 665). As Kerfoot and Knights (1993, p. 672) argue, at the level of embodied experience, this corporate-manager masculinity results

> in the position whereby individuals feel "driven" for no discernible reason, other than as a part of what it means, and how it feels, to subscribe to an ideal of competence, and where the display of vulnerability is to threaten the image of that competence.

This translates into the denial or suppression of emotionality, fear, and uncertainty and, therefore, in the social situation of the off-line caucus, it should not be surprising to find MTI managers unanimously supporting launch; to do otherwise would mean exhibiting fear and uncertainty. These corporate managers displayed, as Rosabeth Moss Kanter (1977, p. 22) states in her discussion of managerial masculinity, "a capacity to set aside personal, emotional considerations in the interests of task accomplishments." Indeed, MTI managers disregarded (at least publicly) during the entire teleconference and off-line caucus the fact that human beings were on *Challenger*. The task was to "get *Challenger* up" and all factors antagonistic to that goal, including human life, were deemed irrelevant.

This professional-managerial class-specific masculine discourse on the part of MTI managers is similar to the "technostrategic" discourse outlined by Carol Cohn (1987, 1995) in her important research on nuclear defense intellectuals. Cohn (1995, pp. 134-135) found that during professional meetings these men systematically suppressed

> the emotional, the concrete, the particular, the human bodies and their vulnerability, human lives and their subjectivity—all of which are marked as feminine in the binary dichotomies of gender discourse. In other words, gender discourse informs and shapes nuclear and national security discourse.

Similarly, MTI managers eschewed any discussion of human beings (the flight crew) and their vulnerability to the risky technology, clearly exhibiting how masculinity in this social situation was constructed in opposition to emphasized femininity. Moreover, it was the class-specific masculine discourse that generated this *indifference* to the human consequences of managerial decisions. In short, being more attentive to the survival of their lucrative contract rather than the survival of human beings was a means of "doing masculinity" as well as "doing class" and, as a result, corporate crime.[14]

The decision to launch by MTI managers can be understood, then, in terms of its captivating and enticing masculine appeal—a social practice that had become normalized in MTI managerial relationships. And because masculinity is constantly renegotiated and "made," voting to launch (and, therefore, changing their earlier no-launch position) was an acceptable (that is accountable) practice for its making in that particular social situation; a practice that "allowed" these managers to live up to a particular class and masculine ideal.

It is tempting to end the analysis here simply by reasoning that risk-taking managerial-masculinity "gave rise" to this corporate crime. Although this conclusion is attractive and not without substance, it disregards the diversity of masculinities actually constructed in corporations and thus their relation to corporate crime. Consequently, we must consider the varieties of masculinities at MTI, not just one type. Indeed, analyzing masculinities places us in a position to address why some men at MTI (engineers), despite the institutionalized and heavy emphasis on risk taking, ardently opposed the launch. It is to the engineers that we now turn.

Resisting Launch

"Of all the major professions," Judy Wajcman (1991, p. 145) writes, "engineering contains the smallest proportion of females" and, like management, "projects a heavily masculine image." Corporate managers validate masculinity by success at securing corporate economic goals whereas engineers are concerned primarily with technical competence/ achievements and tend to devalue economic goals (Cockburn & Ormrod, 1993, p. 161; Vaughan, 1989, p. 337). Indeed, managers and engineers "identify themselves as being in— and 'from'—different 'worlds' " (Dubinskas, 1988, p. 185). Consequently, both managers and engineers weave gendered distinctions into their everyday understanding of "the job," and thus construct masculinity differently.

The relationship between "technical competence" and the social construction of gender difference is well documented in the literature; Cynthia Cockburn (1985, p. 12) states the following: "femininity is incompatible with technological competence; to feel technically competent is to feel manly." Nevertheless, to argue that technical competence is "manly" is not to infer only one type of technical masculinity. Indeed, working class and professional-managerial men construct masculinity differently, depending on their relation to technology in the workplace. For working-class men, the work environment of the shop floor is given significance by associating manual work with a physically strong and active type of masculinity. In other words, the masculinity of the shop floor stresses the presentation and celebration of physical prowess (Cockburn, 1983, 1985; Clatterbaugh, 1990; Willis, 1979).

Professional engineers, however, do not claim physical prowess, but construct masculinity through their possession of abstruse and "expert" technical knowledge (Wajcman, 1991, p. 39). As Cockburn (1985, p. 196) shows, for professional engineers "intellectuality and analytical power are appropriated for masculinity." Wajcman (1991, p. 144) further points out that this knowledge bestows masculine power on engineers: "in relation to other men and women who lack this expertise, in terms of the material rewards this skill brings, and even in terms of their popular portrayal as 'heroes' at the frontiers of technological progress." Thus, technical competence is a key source of masculine power among men and "doing engineering" is simultaneously "doing" a particular type of technically competent masculinity. Indeed, being in control of the very latest technology (such as the space shuttle *Challenger*) "signifies being involved in directing the future" and so is a highly esteemed activity, whereas mastery over other kinds of technology (such as machines on the shop floor) does not accord the same status or power (Wajcman, 1991, pp. 144-145). Professional engineering not only increases for engineers "their sense of the greatness of their sex," but also inculcates "a sense of being special" among the technically competent (Cockburn, 1985, p. 172).

Clearly, then, a major part of professional-engineer masculinity is to be in command of the particular technology and, therefore, to know the limits of that technology. Consequently, these engineers (relative to managers) place very high priority on quality and safety (Starbuck & Milliken, 1988, p. 333). Indeed, Cockburn (1985, pp. 171, 172) stresses the emotional investment engineers lodge in "their" technology:

In the main these men identify themselves with technology and identify technology with masculinity. . . . Engineers identify so closely with the technology with which they are involved that many will choose their employment less by the salary it offers than by the complexity of the technology it opens up to them.

Anticipating Cockburn 20 years earlier, Samuel Florman (1976) emphasized the sensual pleasures secured from "doing engineering" and most recently, Sally Hacker (1989) speaks of a "masculine erotiization of engineering" in which technological innovation is realized as exhilarating and a source of intense pleasure and arousal.

Given this emotional charge, professional engineers have a direct interest in the technology succeeding as planned and, concurrently, technological success delivers a virile status to engineers, thereby ensuring a claim to "engineer masculinity" (Wajcman, 1991). As a result, risk taking is *not* the appealing masculine practice to engineers that it is to managers. Indeed, for engineers, inasmuch as technical failure threatens their masculinity, it should not be surprising that MTI engineers would exhibit greater caution regarding O-ring capability and argue against launch.

Thus, whereas managers see themselves as "realists" struggling with immediate economic crises that sometimes demand risk taking, engineers attempt to protect their work from myopic managers and are more inclined to disdain risk taking (Dubinskas, 1988, p. 201). Indeed, these strikingly different practices were accomplished situationally during the off-line caucus and brilliantly illustrate the relational character of masculinities. They demonstrate how the definition of masculinity is not only the collective work of a group of people, in this case corporate managers and engineers, but is constructed differently (despite similar class standing) through social interaction. Both groups exhibit the different ways masculinity is defined and sustained, and how this proprietary masculinity relates to their definition of work-related issues; managers and engineers actively confront the work situation and shape practices for solving problems. Yet they do this in distinctly different ways, and it is this contrasting social action that is central to the production of different masculinities. From essentially similar starting points, class, race, and gender privilege as well as engagement in "mental labor," two divergent masculinities are produced. Both groups of men share themes of hegemonic masculinity, such as the importance of work in the paid labor market and, clearly, both have benefited from the subordination of women, are white, and members of the professional-managerial class, yet they rework these hegemonic themes in situationally specific ways. Indeed, the notions of "manager" and "engineer" inflects their commonality with difference, unfolding hegemonic masculinity into its diverse parts.[15]

In addition, the *relationship* between these masculinities is in part the basis of MTI organization. As with other male-dominated organizations, such as the military—general/soldier (Connell, 1995b) and the police—office cop/street cop (Messerschmidt, 1993), it is the relationship between engineer and manager masculinities, technically competent but subordinate to managerial authority on one hand, dominating and economically competent on the other, that is in part the foundation of MTI organization. Yet as indicated, this relationship is far from one of simple complementarity but rather is embedded in a power hierarchy.[16] At MTI a difference in hegemonic masculinities was constructed in practice by the asymmetry of power between managers and engineers. "Decisions" were ultimately in the hands of management, yet as we have seen, the power to manage is not always easily exercised. Engineers can and do wield the weapon of "technical competence," at least to some degree, to make their collective voice heard. During the off-line caucus, two MTI engineers attempted to protect "their technology" by challenging managerial authority. There was a contest of hegemonic masculinities in which both managers and engineers were attempting to control the SRB technology. Nevertheless, there are limits to oppositional practices by the less powerful, as noted by the engineers themselves. For example, Boisjoly stated to the President's Commission (1986, p. 1421): "I had my say, and I never take any management right to take the input of an engineer and then make a decision based on that input, and I truly believe that." Similarly, Brian Russell, another MTI engineer, told the Commission (p. 1487), "It was a management decision at the vice president's level, and they had heard all they could hear, and I felt there was nothing more to say."[17]

What these statements reveal is that power is a relationship that structures social interaction between men in the corporation. By engaging in practices that reproduce the division of labor and power, managers and engineers are not only doing their job and, therefore, reproducing corporate organization, they are also constructing differing hegemonic masculinities. Both managers and engineers are acknowledging through practice that the lopsided power relationships are indeed "fair."

In addition, the comment by Jerry Mason to Bob Lund during the off-line caucus, to take off your "engineering hat" and put on your "management hat," is key to understanding the social construction of, and relationship between, masculinities. Lund was vice president of engineering, making him both an engineer and a manager. Initially, Lund put on his engineering hat and argued against launch. Once he entered the social situation of the off-line caucus, however, Lund followed instructions, put on his management hat, and concurred with the other managers to approve launch.

What this reveals is that through the exchange of hats, Lund reestablished a corporate-manager masculinity that had been diminished by his earlier opposition to launch. The problem for Lund was to produce configurations of behavior that could be seen by others as normative. Yet, as the social setting changed, from outside to inside the caucus, so did the conceptualization of what is normative masculine behavior. In short, Lund formed different types of hegemonic masculinity that could be assessed and approved in both social settings as normal.

The case of Lund demonstrates how we maintain different gender identities that may be emphasized or avoided, depending on the social setting. Men construct their gendered action in relation to how such actions might be interpreted by others (that is, their accountability) in the particular social context in which they occur. Given the power relation prevalent in the off-line caucus, Lund did hegemonic masculinity differently because the setting and the available resources changed.[18]

Overall, the disparate degree of power among men significantly impacts the varieties of masculinities constructed and therefore support for, or rejection of, the launch as a resource for doing masculinity.

Engineers were able to oppose the launch because such a practice was, in this particular situation, a resource for doing gender; attempting to prevent the launch was an accountable practice for doing professional-engineer masculinity. Thus, MTI managers (including Lund) advocated an unsafe launch, whereas engineers resisted such a launch, because of different masculine meanings attaching to the particular practice.

Conclusion

Gender is one of the most significant ways we make sense of our daily work environment and work in the paid labor market is a crucial milieu for the construction of masculinities. Both managers and engineers construct hegemonic masculinity at the workplace, but the way in which they do so reveals a fundamental difference. And this diversity is strikingly apparent in support for or rejection of the *Challenger* launch. Indeed, as David Morgan (1992, p. 86) argues, the kind of work determines "the material out of which certain masculinities are shaped." The corporation sets limits for the type of masculinities that might be constructed and one's position in the corporate division of labor and power determines the resources available for masculine practices. The *Challenger* illustration reveals how the corporate division of labor and power is constituted by social action and, in turn, provides class and occupational resources for doing masculinity. In this way social structures both constrain and enable social action and, therefore, masculinities and corporate crime. In short, the data on the space shuttle *Challenger* explosion shows how in the same social situation, one type of hegemonic masculinity (manager) was constructed through the commission of corporate crime whereas contemporaneously another type of hegemonic masculinity (engineer) was constructed through resisting that crime.

Thus, managers and engineers experience their corporate world from a specific position in the organization and, accordingly, construct hegemonic masculinity in a uniquely appropriate way. Indeed, conceptualizing the *Challenger* explosion from a structured action perspective demonstrates that we are able now to explore sociologically which males commit which crimes in which social situations; in other words, why some men in corporations "manage to kill" whereas other men do not.

Notes

1. The report of the President's Commission provides the most thorough documentation of the events and decisions that led to the launch, and serves here as the primary data on the explosion.

2. I agree with Thorsten Sellin (1938) who long ago criticized criminologists for limiting their investigations to violations of the law. For Sellin (p. 23), such a definition of crime disregards a fundamental criterion of science: "the scientist must have the freedom to define his [or her] own terms." In other words, criminologists should not be restricted in their research simply to violations of legal precedents. Consequently, although no one involved in the decision to launch *Challenger* was criminalized by the state, following Beirne and Messerschmidt (1995, p. 22) I label this act "corporate crime" because it conforms to the following definition: "Corporate crime is any illegal, socially injurious act of intent and/or indifference that occurs for the purpose of furthering corporate goals, and that physically and/or economically abuses individuals in the United States, abroad, or both." As I show in this chapter, although the killing of the seven crew members was not intentional, it clearly was a socially injurious act of indifference that occurred for the purpose of furthering corporate goals.

3. McConnell (1987, p. 40) states the following:

They decided that the strap-on solid fuel boosters would be equipped with large parachutes to carry them to a soft water landing 100 miles downrange from the launch site after their fuel was spent. The huge external tank would be sacrificed after use. But the orbiter would glide back to a shuttle landing field near its launch site, be mated with a new fuel tank and refurbished solid rocket boosters, and be ready for flight again within 2 weeks.

4. A December 12, 1973, NASA selection board report stated the following (cited in President's Commission, 1986, p. 120):

Thiokol's cost advantages were substantial and consistent throughout all areas evaluated. . . . The Thiokol motor case joints used dual O-rings and test ports between seals, enabling a simple leak check without pressurizing the entire motor. This innovative design feature increased reliability and decreased operations at the launch site, indicating good attention to low cost (design, development, testing, and engineering) and production. . . . Thiokol could do a more economical job than any of the other proposers in both the development and the production phases of the program.

5. MTI engineers based their SRB design on the Air Force's Titan III model. Because, however, the Titan had experienced occasional erosion of its single O-ring design, MTI engineers adopted a second, presumably redundant O-ring arrangement into each joint, to hypothetically make the *Challenger* safer.

6. Early tests performed between 1977 and 1980 showed that during the initial period of launch, pressure surge "joint rotation" occurred, causing the secondary O-ring to become completely disengaged from its sealing surface (President's Commission, 1986, pp. 122-123). Moreover, the orbital test flight series, which consisted of four flights from April 1981 to July 1982, repeatedly evinced O-ring erosion caused by "joint rotation." For example, after the third test flight, inspection revealed "that joint rotation caused the loss of the secondary O-ring as a backup seal," which could ultimately result in a "loss of mission vehicle and crew due to metal erosion, burn through, and probable case burst resulting in fire and deflagration" (pp. 125-126).

7. Vaughan (1994) provides an interesting discussion of how managers and engineers jointly defined the SRB joints an "acceptable risk." She fails to acknowledge and analyze, however, the engineers changing position, especially the necessity of fixing the erosion problem prior to future flights. I examine this turnabout next.

8. The President's Commission (1986, p. 148) would subsequently agree with Boisjoly, stating that the O-ring erosion history presented to MTI management by the engineers "was sufficiently detailed to require corrective action prior to the next flight."

9. As Bob Lund, vice president of engineering at MTI, stated in testimony to the President's Commission (1986, pp. 1456-1457): "We have dealt with Marshall for a long time and have always been in the position of defending our position that we were ready to fly . . . [now] we had to prove to them we *weren't* ready." And as Roger Boisjoly (p. 1421) put it: "This was a meeting where the determination was to launch, and it was up to us to prove beyond a shadow of a doubt that it was not safe to do so.

This is in total reversal to what the position usually is in a preflight conversation."

10. Due to space limitations I concentrate my analysis in the remaining sections exclusively on the corporate (MTI) decision to launch.

11. The importance of risk taking in the corporate-managerial world was recently highlighted in a book on women managers. According to Driscoll and Goldberg (1993, p. 46), to gain entry to the masculine corporate-managerial "club," "women would do well to become risk takers" because "risk taking pays off . . . the greater the risk, the greater the reward."

12. The sociology of risk literature has shockingly ignored this important link with gender. See, for example, Short and Clarke (1992) and Luhman (1993).

13. It should therefore not be surprising to find that interview data of corporate managers shows that they "care about their reputations for risk taking and are eager to expound on their sentiments about the deficiencies of others" (March & Shapira, 1987, p. 1413).

14. Bob Lund, vice president of engineering at MTI, stated the following to the President's Commission (1986, p. 1459) when asked why he initially opposed launch: "You know this program has people on it, and so I am very concerned about that, and I want to make sure that if there is any hint of a problem, that we are not extending that." He is the only person, however, to acknowledge such a concern to the Commission, there is *no* evidence he announced this concern at any time during the launch decision process and, finally, he eventually voted, with the other managers, to launch *Challenger*. Thus, although MTI managers did not intend harm to the seven crew members, they clearly were indifferent to the human consequences of their actions and, therefore, committed corporate crime (see the definition of corporate crime in Note 2). Moreover, I must stress that it was the gendered interaction and discourse within the particular social situation of the teleconference and off-line caucus that generated this indifference.

15. It is important to note again the historical nature of hegemonic masculinity. As stated here and in the Prologue, hegemonic masculinity currently is characterized by whiteness, work in the paid labor market, the subordination of women, professional-managerial class, and heterosexism. Yet this is different from hegemonic masculinity during slavery. As pointed out in Chapter 1, hegemonic masculinity constituted at that time whiteness; heading a family; ownership of land, slaves, or both; literacy; and participation in political affairs.

16. Due to space limitations I am able to consider only power relations at MTI. We also observe power relations, however, between managers of the two organizations. MTI's reversal from a no-launch to a launch decision clearly must be understood in terms of its relatively powerless position vis-a-vis Marshall. That is, MTI must be responsive to its major customer or potentially suffer dire economic consequences. Marshall managers, by reason of their powerful position, had the resources to pressure MTI to prove it was unsafe to launch. Thus, in relation to Marshall managers, MTI managers experienced a subordinate position; in relation to their engineers they realized a powerful position. This indicates how power and powerlessness are not absolutes but rather shift according to context and social situation. Consequently, a full understanding of the power dynamics involved in this event, something clearly beyond the scope of this book, must consider this relationship between the "men at Marshall" and the "men at MTI."

17. This comment by Brian Russell indicates that the two engineers, Roger Boisjoly and Arnie Thompson, who challenged the authority of management during the off-line caucus were acting as spokespersons for the other eight engineers.

18. Lund simply was not "jumping" from one masculinity to another. To "do" manager masculinity in this setting required Lund to actively demasculinize what had previously been an acceptable masculine practice for him (opposing the launch). When asked by the President's Commission (1986, pp. 1568-1569) why he changed his mind when he changed his hat, Lund responded by supporting Mulloy's gendered dichotomy discussed previously: irrational/qualitative (wimpish) versus rational/quantitative (masculine). In short, by supporting the launch Lund was able to patently separate himself from what the particular situation of the caucus defined as "wimpish" and, therefore, be assessed as normatively masculine.

Epilogue

Summary Thoughts
and Future Directions

The case studies empirically illuminate the basic elements of structured action theory: To understand crime we must appreciate how structure and action are woven inextricably in the ongoing activity of "doing" gender, race, and class. Structured-action theory (as applied here in a variety of historical and social settings) defines the two crucial components for understanding crime:

1. *Inseparability of structure and action.*
   Social structures are realized only through social action and social action requires structure as its condition.

2. *Situational salience of "doing" gender, race, and class.*
   Gender, race, and class are not absolutes and are not equally significant in every social setting where crime is realized. That is, depending on the social setting, accountability to certain categories is more salient than accountability to other categories.

Nevertheless, to foster understanding of crime as structured action requires novel forms of research. Thus, in this Epilogue, I briefly sketch ways in which structured action theory can be developed further through new empirical work. In short, I believe the framework of structured action theory provides concepts relevant to a variety of methodological approaches, from historical and documentary research to ethnographies and life histories. Indeed, the accomplishment of varieties of gender, race, class, and crime are situated in history, and their meanings change over time. Thus, a key element of future research is to trace the historical transformation and difference among gender, race, class, and crime. For example, Chapter 1 shows that Reconstruction created a new social connect in which an alarmist ideology about African American male sexuality was constructed and resulted in a pronounced public mob violence employed by white supremacist men. During this period race and gender (but not class) grew particularly salient to actuating crime: White supremacist men constructed a specific type of whiteness and hegemonic masculinity through the practice of lynching.

We need much more historical research of this kind to understand further the relationship among differing social relations and when specific relationships effect crime more saliently than others. Such research will not only provide insight on the past, but help us comprehend how we have reached the present.

Similarly, using written documents, such as archival sources, criminal justice records, and government reports, for investigation is an excellent method of obtaining information on gender, race, class, and crime. For example, in Chapter 4, the report of the Presidential Commission served as the primary data on the explosion of the space shuttle *Challenger*. By drawing on the testimony of the men involved in the launch decision, I was able to develop a rich and detailed description of the events leading up to launch, as well as the masculine interaction in the "corporate boardroom" during the off-line caucus.

Moreover, when the research has a specific historical dimension, such as during Reconstruction, written documents are essential. Thus, testimony from government documents cited in Chapter 1 contributed immense insight into the gender and race meanings of lynching during this time period.

All research methods have their advantages and limitations, but arguably one of the most valuable qualitative methods for investigating how structured action is intertwined with "doing" gender, race, class, and crime, is the life-history study.[1]

Life-History Studies

The life-history method never realized the sociological distinction Thomas and Znaniecki (1958) expected when they announced that the life story constituted the "perfect" type of sociological material. Nonetheless, although the method has remained on the margins of sociological and criminological acceptability since its heyday at the Chicago School (Plummer, 1983), it has experienced a resurgence in both the sociology of masculinities (Connell, 1995a) and criminology (Sampson & Laub, 1993). Such revival is due, in part, to the fact that life histories tap the continuous "lived experience" of individuals. That is, the method necessitates a close consideration of the meaning of social life for those who enact it, revealing *their* experiences, meanings, practices, and social world.

But in addition to in-depth documentation of one's conceptual world and the representations of such conceptions through practice, the life history links these with the social and historical context in which they are embedded. As Connell (1995a, p. 89) points out:

> The project that is documented in a life-history story is itself the relation between the social conditions that determine practice and the future social world that practice brings into being. That is to say, life-history method always concerns the making of social life through time. It is literally history.

Thus, the life-history method is an important research tool for studying the inseparability of structure and action, "doing" gender, race, class, and crime, as well as individual and structural social change. No other social research method provides as much detail about social development and change as does the life-history study of social practices over time. Chapter 2 explored the changes in Malcolm X's masculine identity within a range of race and class social contexts: a childhood in which he constantly battled for acceptance as a young man; a zoot suit culture that embraced him without stigma as a "hipster" and "hustler"; and finally a spiritual and political movement that celebrated him as father, husband, and national spokesperson. Across these sites and through the shifting currencies of his sense of gender, race, and class identity, Malcolm moved in and out of crime. Malcolm simply appropriated crime as a resource for "doing masculinity" at a specific moment in his life, a period when gender, race, and class relations were equally significant. In this way, the life-history method provides data not only about why people engage in crime at certain stages of their lives, but how that engagement relates to the salience of various combinations of gender, race, and class.

Moreover, the life-history method provides considerable insight as to when and why people abandon criminal practices. In particular, I highlighted the case of Malcolm X as an example of how the increasing significance of a new social situation combined with a growing race consciousness contributed significantly to Malcolm's desistance from crime.

Accordingly, Chapter 2 suggests that a structured action criminology conducted within a life-history methodology may open significant avenues for answering the never ending questions on both the *causes* of harmful behavior and how to *control* them. In particular, I urge life-history studies not only on the relationship between crime and masculinities but on the relationships between crime and femininities, race, class, sexualities, and institutions. Let us briefly look at each of these areas.

Femininities, Race, and Class

Given that gender is a relational concept, it follows logically that to understand masculinities we must understand simultaneously the social construction of femininities and vice versa. Thus we gain not only an interrelational understanding of gender, but we increase substantially our comprehension of men, women, and crime. Notwithstanding the feminist-inspired criminological research on girls and women over the past 20 years, there remain several areas in which the distinctive activities of girls and women require greater study. In particular, there is a need for extensive research on the historical and contemporary constructions of femininities and their relation to crime. Chapter 3 argues that gender, race, and class are equally significant for contemporary gang girls; that violent interaction with other young street women is a means for constructing a specific race, class, and feminine identity. Participating in the specific social situation of the gang, these girls use available race and class resources not to construct masculinity but a particular type of femininity. Thus, Chapter 3 challenges notions of conceptualizing violence by women as simplistically "unnatural," "deviant," and "masculine," and points both to the importance of ongoing investigation of gender *differences* in crime and to gender *similarities* in crime. Certainly, then, one of the future explanatory tasks of structured action theory is to explore varieties of femininities, crime, and social control.

The preceding discussion of femininities and crime sensitizes criminologists to a similar need for research on race. When race is discussed in relation to crime, invariably it is African American crime, which marginalizes other people of color. Fortunately, structured action theory, because it is not exclusively a theory of "gender and crime," provides the necessary eclectic approach. Indeed, as argued throughout this book, structured action theory generates concepts relevant to research on gender, race, class, and crime. Nevertheless, the significance of each social relation shifts with changing contexts: In one situation both gender and race may be important factors for actuating crime (Chapter 1); in other settings gender, race, and class all may be relevant (Chapters 2 and 3); or simply class and gender may be significant (Chapter 4). Moreover, these chapters reflect that any combination of the three relations can be pertinent to understanding motivation for crime. Although I concentrated in this book on gender and crime (in particular, masculinities and crime), there is a long-standing need for research on when accountability to race alone becomes more salient than accountability to other categories for actuating crime. For example, other than Chapter 1, I know of no other research that examines the historical and/or contemporary constructions of varieties of *whiteness* and their relation to crime. In short, structured action theory provides the means to subdivide race

(Chapter 3), like gender and class, into diverse categories that enable an examination, for instance, of the relation between various types of "whiteness" and crime.

For some time, criminologists have examined differences in crime among classes—in particular, middle-class (white-collar crime) versus working-class (street crime). Yet, as with race, what has gone unnoticed by theory and, therefore, research are the diverse definitions and practices of "class" within each of these categories, their relation to crime, and how these definitions and practices affect "doing" gender and race. The Chapter 4 examination of the *Challenger* launch decision revealed the salience of class and gender (but not race) for actuating corporate crime. In addition, however, the launch decision-making evidence provides the opportunity to separate the professional-managerial class category into two hegemonic masculine constructions. That is, both managers and engineers constructed a specific type of hegemonic masculinity, yet did so differently through the occupational resources available to each. Managerial masculinity was constructed through the commission of corporate crime; contemporaneously, engineer masculinity was constructed through resisting that crime. Therefore, in the same class and gender setting, we could discern which men committed corporate crime and which did not—and why.

In short, we need research on *diversity* in the social construction of gender, race, class, and crime.

Sexualities and Institutions

Over the last 20 years, an important and sophisticated historical scholarship has demonstrated that sexuality is socially constructed and not biologically ordained. That is, sexualities are constructed in historically specific social practices. Accordingly, sexuality varies not only from society to society but within societies themselves. Sexuality is not a biological constant but a product of human agency (Messerschmidt, 1993).

In addition, societies define who are "appropriate" partners and what are the "appropriate" sexual practices. These definitions provide the permissions, prohibitions, limits, and possibilities with which erotica and desire are constructed (Messerschmidt, 1993). The result is that subordinated sexualities are ridiculed and repressed and, thus, construct difference. In the example of lynching during Reconstruction (Chapter 1), we observe how conceptions of sexuality, in combination with other social relations such as race, are employed historically to divide men by creating difference and a power hierarchy among them.

Similarly, gay bashing provides a contemporary example of employing conceptions of sexuality to "divide and conquer" Other men. Thus, to better understand sexual violence against women and men as well as criminalized forms of consensual sex (e.g., prostitution), we need to bring criminology "out of the closet" by supporting extensive historical and contemporary research on the relationship among sexualities, gender, race, class, and crime.

Chapter 4 revealed that gender, race, and class are not simply the practices of individuals, but are likewise the province of social institutions. Indeed, it is the institutionalization of gender, race, and class relations that serves to reproduce social structures of labor, power, and sexuality. Accordingly, we must scrutinize and analyze such institutional settings as the workplace, family, school, and state. And within these settings we must examine the particular and varying socially constructed combinations of gender, race, class, and crime, as well as examine how these categories are related to social-control practices by, for example, the police, courts, and prisons.

In conclusion, I recommend these as the chief areas of focus for those working within a structured action framework. All such studies seek to engage the demanding empirical inquiries that confidently will lead to theoretical reappraisal and, inevitably, to advances in structured action theory.

Note

1. Ferrell and Sanders (1995b, p. 305) argued recently that survey research and quantitative analysis are of "little use" to criminology because "their illusions of precise objectivity mask an inherent and imposed imprecision" as well as a characteristic inability to explore the situated meanings, symbolism, and "interpersonal style in the lived experiences of

everyday criminality." Once these "old methodologies" are demystified, they go on, what remains is the ethnographic case study because such methodology is designed "to unravel the phenomenological foreground of criminality" (p. 306). I obviously agree with Ferrell and Sanders, simply adding a "life-history immersion" to their call for an "ethnographic immersion."

References

Acker, J. (1990). Hierarchies, jobs, bodies: A theory of gendered organizations. *Gender and Society, 4*(2), 139-158.

Acker, J. (1992). Gendering organizational theory. In A. J. Mills and P. Tancred (Eds.), *Gendering organizational analysis* (pp. 248-260). Newbury Park, CA: Sage.

Adler, F. (1975). *Sisters in crime.* New York: McGraw-Hill.

Adler, F. (1977). The interaction between women's emanicaption and female criminality: A cross-cultural perspective. *International Journal of Criminology and Penology, 5*(1), 101-112.

Arch, E. C. (1993). Risk-taking: A Motivational basis for sex differences. *Psychological Reports, 73*(2), 3-11.

Allen, J. (1989). Men, crime, and criminology: Recasting the questions. *International Journal of the Sociology of Law, 17*(1), 19-39.

Ashbury, H. (1927). *The gangs of New York.* New York: Capricorn.

Ayers, E. L. (1984). *Vengeance and justice: Crime and punishment in the 19th-century American South.* New York: Oxford University Press.

Baker, P. (1984). The domestication of politics: Women and American political society, 1780-1920. *American Historical Review, 89*(June), 620-647.

Bedau, H. A., & Radelet, M. L. (1987). Miscarriages of justice in potentially capital cases. *Stanford Law Review, 40*(1), 21-98.

Bederman, G. (1995). *Manliness and civilization: A cultural history of gender and race in the United States, 1880-1917.* Chicago: University of Chicago Press.

Beirne, P., & Messerschmidt, J. W. (1995). *Criminology* (2nd ed.). San Diego, CA: Harcourt Brace.

Bennett, J. (1981). *Oral history and delinquency: The rhetoric of criminology*. Chicago: University of Chicago Press.

Boisjoly, R. M. (1987, December). *Ethical decisions: Morton Thiokol and the space shuttle* Challenger *disaster*. Paper presented at the annual meeting of the American Society of Mechanical Engineers, Boston, MA.

Brown, R. M. (1975). *Strain of violence: Historical studies of American violence and vigilantism*. New York: Oxford University Press.

Brundage, W. F. (1993). *Lynching in the new South: Georgia and Virginia, 1880-1930*. Chicago: University of Illinois Press.

Campbell, A. (1987). Self definition by rejection: The case of gang girls. *Social Problems, 34*(5), 451-466.

Campbell, A. (1990). Female participation in gangs. In C. R. Huff (Ed.), *Gangs in America* (pp. 163-182). Newbury Park: Sage.

Campbell, A. (1991). *The girls in the gang*. Cambridge, MA: Basil Blackwell. (Original work published 1984)

Campbell, A. (1993). *Men, women, and aggression*. New York: Basic Books.

Carrington, K. (1993). *Offending girls*. Sydney: Allen & Unwin.

Chesney-Lind, M. (1993). Girls, gangs, and violence: Anatomy of a backlash. *Humanity and Society, 17*(3), 321-344.

Chesney-Lind, M., & Shelden, R. G. (1992). *Girls, delinquency and juvenile justice*. Belmont, CA: Wadsworth.

Chibnall, S. (1985). Whistle and zoot: The changing meaning of a suit of clothes. *History Workshop Journal, 20*(Fall), 56-81.

Clatterbaugh, K. (1990). *Contemporary perspectives on masculinity*. Boulder, CO: Westview.

Cockburn, C. (1983). *Brothers: Male dominance and technological change*. London: Pluto.

Cockburn, C. (1985). *Machinery of dominance: Women, men, and technical knowhow*. London: Pluto.

Cockburn, C., & Ormrod, S. (1993). *Gender and technology in the making*. Newbury Park, CA: Sage.

Cohn, C. (1987). Sex and death in the rational world of defense intellectuals. *Signs, 12*(4), 687-718.

Cohn, C. (1995). Wars, wimps, and women: Talking gender and thinking war. In M. S. Kimmel & M. A. Messner (Eds.), *Men's lives* (pp. 131-143). Boston: Allyn & Bacon.

Collins, P. H. (1992). Learning to think for ourselves: Malcolm X's black nationalism reconsidered. In J. Wood (Ed.), *Malcolm X: In our own image* (pp. 59-85). New York: St. Martin's.

The condition of affairs in the late insurrectionary states: Report and testimony to the Joint Select Committee. 42d Cong., 2d Sess. 13 (1871).

Connell, R. W. (1987). *Gender and power: Society, the person, and sexual politics*. Stanford, CA: Stanford University Press.

Connell, R. W. (1995a). *Masculinities*. Berkeley: University of California Press.

Connell, R. W. (1995b). Masculinity, violence, and war. In M. S. Kimmel & M. A. Messner (Eds.), *Men's lives* (pp. 125-130). Boston: Allyn & Bacon.

Cosgrove, S. (1984). The zoot suit and style warfare. *Radical America, 18*(1), 38-51.

Cullen, J. (1992). "I's a man now": Gender and African American men. In C. Clinton & N. Silber (Eds.), *Divided houses: Gender and the Civil War* (pp. 76-91). New York: Oxford University Press.

Daly, K., & Chesney-Lind, M. (1988). Feminism and criminology. *Justice Quarterly, 5*(4), 497-538.

Davis, A. (1983). *Women, race, and class*. New York: Vintage.

DeKeseredy, W. S., & Schwartz, M. D. (1993). Male peer support and woman abuse. *Sociological Spectrum, 13*(4), 393-413.

D'Emilio, J., & Freedman, E. B. (1988). *Intimate matters: A history of sexuality in America*. New York: Harper & Row.

Devor, H. (1987). Gender-blending females: Women and sometimes men. *American Behavioral Scientist, 31*(1), 12-40.

Donaldson, M. (1993). What is hegemonic masculinity? *Theory and Society, 22*, 643-657.

Dowd Hall, J. (1979). *Revolt against chivalry: Jessie Daniel Ames and the women's campaign against lynching*. New York: Columbia University Press.

Dowd Hall, J. (1983). "The mind that burns in each body": Women, rape, and racial violence. In A. Snitow, C. Stansill, & S. Thompson (Eds.), *Powers of desire: The politics of sexuality* (pp. 328-49). New York: Monthly Review Press.

Driscoll, D. M., & Goldberg, C. R. (1993). *Members of the club: The coming of age of executive women*. New York: Free Press.

Dubinskas, F. A. (1988). Janus organizations: Scientists and managers in genetic engineering firms. In F. A. Dubinskas, (Ed.), *Making time: Ethnographies of high-technology organizations* (pp. 170-232). Philadelphia: Temple University Press.

Faith, K. (1993). *Unruly women*. Vancouver, BC: Press Gang Publishers.

Ferguson, A. (1991). *Sexual democracy: Women, oppression, and revolution*. Boulder, CO: Westview.

Ferrell, J. (1995). Style matters: Criminal identity and social control. In J. Ferrell & C. R. Sanders (Eds.), *Cultural criminology* (pp. 169-189). Boston: Northeastern University Press.

Ferrell, J., & Sanders, C. R. (1995a). Culture, crime, and criminology. In J. Ferrell & C. R. Sanders (Eds.), *Cultural criminology* (pp. 3-21). Boston: Northeastern University Press.

Ferrell, J., & Sanders, C. R. (1995b). Toward a cultural criminology. In J. Ferrell & C. R. Sanders (Eds.), *Cultural criminology* (pp. 297-326). Boston: Northeastern University Press.

Fishman, L. T. (1988, November). *The vice queens: An ethnographic study of black female gang behavior.* Paper presented at the annual meeting of the American Society of Criminology, Chicago, IL.

Florman, S. C. (1976). *The existential pleasures of engineering.* New York: St. Martin's.

Foner, E. (1988). *Reconstruction: America's unfinished revolution, 1863-1877.* New York: Harper & Row.

Fox-Genovese, E. (1988). *Within the plantation household: Black and white women of the old South.* Chapel Hill: University of North Carolina Press.

Fraiman, S. (1994). Geometries of race and gender: Eve Sedgwick, Spike Lee, and Charlayne Hunter-Gault. *Feminist Studies, 20*(1), 67-84.

Frankenberg, R. (1993). *White women, race matters: The social construction of whiteness.* Minneapolis: University of Minnesota Press.

Friedman, S. S. (1995). Beyond white and other: Relationality and narratives of race in feminist discourse. *Signs, 21*(1), 1-49.

Genovese, E. (1974). *Roll, Jordan, roll: The world the slaves made.* New York: Random House.

Giddens, A. (1976). *New rules of sociological method: A positive critique of interpretive sociologies.* New York: Basic Books.

Giddens, A. (1984). *The constitution of society: Outline of the theory of structuration.* Berkeley: University of California Press.

Giddens, A. (1989). A reply to my critics. In D. Held & J. B. Thompson (Eds.), *Social theory of modern societies: Anthony Giddens and his critics* (pp. 249-301). New York: Cambridge University Press.

Gilroy, P. (1990). One nation under a groove: The cultural politics of "race" and racism in Britain. In D. T. Goldberg (Ed.), *Anatomy of racism* (pp. 263-282). Minneapolis: University of Minnesota Press.

Ginzburg, R. (1988). *100 years of lynchings.* Baltimore: Black Classic.

Glenn, E. N. (1992). From servitude to service work: Historical continuities in the racial division of paid reproductive labor. *Signs, 18*(1), 1-43.

Hacker, S. (1989). *Pleasure, power, and technology: Some tales of gender, engineering, and the cooperative workplace.* Boston: Unwin Hyman.

Hagedorn, J. (1988). *People and folks: Gangs, crime, and the underclass in a rustbelt city.* Chicago: Lake View.

Harris, M. G. (1988). *Cholas: Latino girls and gangs*. New York: AMS Press.

Harris, T. (1984). *Exorcising blackness*. Bloomington: Indiana University Press.

Hebdige, D. (1978). *Subculture: The meaning of style*. New York: Routledge.

Hodes, M. E. (1991). *Sex across the color line: White women and black men in the 19th-century American South*. Unpublished doctoral dissertation, Princeton University, Princeton, NJ.

hooks, b. (1984). *Feminist theory: From margin to center*. Boston: South End.

Horton, J. O. (1993). *Free people of color: Inside the African American community*. Washington, DC: Smithsonian Institution Press.

Joe, K., & Chesney-Lind, M. (1993, October). *"Just every mother's angel": An analysis of gender and ethnic variations in youth gang membership*. Paper presented at the annual meeting of the American Society of Criminology, Phoenix, AZ.

Johnston, J. H. (1970). *Race relations and miscegenation in the South, 1776-1860*. Amherst: University of Massachusetts Press.

Jones, J. (1986). *Labor of love, labor of sorrow: Black women, work, and the family from slavery to the present*. New York: Vintage.

Jordan, W. D. (1968). *White over black: American attitudes toward the Negro, 1550-1812*. Chapel Hill: University of North Carolina Press.

Kanter, R. M. (1977). *Men and women of the corporation*. New York: Basic Books.

Katz, J. (1988). *Seductions of crime: Moral and sensual attractions in doing evil*. New York: Basic Books.

Kelley, R. D. G. (1992). The riddle of the zoot: Malcolm Little and black cultural politics during World War II. In J. Wood (Ed.), *Malcolm X: In our own image* (pp. 155-182). New York: St. Martin's.

Kerfoot, D., & Knights, D. (1993). Management, masculinity, and manipulation: From paternalism to corporate strategy in financial services in Britain. *Journal of Management Studies, 30*(4), 659-677.

Kimmel, M. S. (1987). Men's responses to feminism at the turn of the century. *Gender and Society, 1*(3), 261-283.

Kramer, R. C. (1992). The space shuttle *Challenger* explosion: A case study of state-corporate crime. In K. Schlegel & D. Weisburg (Eds.), *White-collar crime reconsidered* (pp. 214-243). Boston: Northeastern University Press.

Lauderback, D., Hansen, J., & Waldorf, D. (1992). "Sisters are doin' it for themselves": A black female gang in San Francisco. *Gang Journal, 1*(2), 57-72.

Luhman, N. (1993). *Risk: A sociological theory*. New York: Aldine.

Malcolm X with Alex Haley. (1964). *The autobiography of Malcolm X.* New York: Ballantine.

Mann, C. R. (1993). Sister against sister: Female intrasexual homicide. In C. C. Culliver (Ed.), *Female criminality: The state of the art* (pp. 195-223). New York: Garland.

Marable, M. (1991). *Race, reform, and rebellion: The second reconstruction in Black America, 1945-1990.* Jackson: University Press of Mississippi.

March, J. G., & Shapira, Z. (1987). Managerial perspectives on risk and risk taking. *Management Science, 33*(11), 1404-1418.

Martin, S., & Jurik, N. (1996). *Doing justice, doing gender.* Thousand Oaks, CA: Sage.

McConnell, M. (1987). *Challenger: A major malfunction.* Garden City, NY: Doubleday.

Messerschmidt, J. W. (1993). *Masculinities and crime: Critique and reconceptualization of theory.* Lanham, MD: Rowman and Littlefield.

Messner, M. (1995). Boyhood, organized sports, and the construction of masculinities. In M. S. Kimmel & M. A. Messner (Eds.), *Men's lives* (pp. 102-114). Boston: Allyn & Bacon.

Moore, J. (1991). *Going down to the Barrio: Homeboys and homegirls in Change.* Philadelphia: Temple University Press.

Morgan, D. H. J. (1992). *Discovering men.* New York: Routledge.

Morgen, S. (1990). Conceptualizing and changing consciousness: Socialist feminist perspectives. In K. V. Hansen & I. J. Philipson (Eds.), *Women, class, and the feminist imagination: A socialist feminist reader* (pp. 277-291). Philadelphia: Temple University Press.

Naffine, N. (1987). *Female crime: The construction of women in criminology.* Boston: Allen and Unwin.

Naffine, N. (Ed.). (1995). *Gender, crime, and feminism.* Brookfield, MA: Dartmouth.

Newburn, T., & Stanko, E. (Eds.). (1994). *Just boys doing business? Men, masculinities, and crime.* London: Routledge.

Pinkney, A. (1976). *Red, black, and green: Black nationalism in the United States.* New York: Cambridge University Press.

Plummer, K. (1983). *Documents of life.* Boston: Allen and Unwin.

President's Commission. (1986). *Report of the presidential commission on the space shuttle* Challenger *accident.* Washington, DC: Government Printing Office.

Quicker, J. (1983). *Homegirls: Characterizing Chicana gangs.* San Pedro, CA: International Universities Press.

Rable, G. C. (1984). *But there was no peace: The role of violence in the politics of reconstruction.* Athens: University of Georgia Press.

Raper, A. F. (1969). *The tragedy of lynching.* New York: Negro University Press.

Rubin, G. (1984). Thinking sex: Notes for a radical theory of the politics of sexuality. In C. E. Vance (Ed.), *Pleasure and danger: Exploring female sexuality* (pp. 267-319). Boston: Routledge.

Russett, C. E. (1989). *Sexual science: The Victorian construction of womanhood.* Cambridge, MA: Harvard University Press.

Sampson, R. J., & Laub, J. H. (1993). *Crime in the making: Pathways and turning points through life.* Cambridge, MA: Harvard University Press.

Schwarz, P. J. (1988). *Twice condemned: Slaves and the criminal laws of Virginia, 1705-1865.* Baton Rouge: Louisiana State University.

Schwendinger, H., & Schwendinger, J. (1985). *Adolescent subcultures and delinquency.* New York: Praeger.

Scott, A. F. (1970). *The Southern lady: From pedestal to politics, 1830-1930.* Chicago: University of Chicago Press.

Segal, L. (1990). *Slow motion: Changing masculinities, changing men.* New Brunswick, NJ: Rutgers University Press.

Sellin, T. (1938). *Culture conflict and crime.* New York: Social Science Research Council.

Shaw, C. (1930). *The jack-roller: A delinquent boy's own story.* Chicago: University of Chicago Press.

Shaw, M. (1995). Conceptualizing violence by women. In R. E. Dobash, R. P. Dobash, & L. Noaks (Eds.), *Gender and crime* (pp. 115-131). Cardiff: University of Wales Press.

Short, J. F., & Clarke, L. (Eds.). (1992). *Organizations, uncertainties, and risk.* Boulder, CO: Westview.

Simpson, S. S. (1991). Caste, class, and violent crime: Explaining difference in female offending. *Criminology, 29*(1), 115-135.

Smith-Rosenberg, C. (1985). *Disorderly conduct: Visions of gender in Victorian America.* New York: Oxford University Press.

Sommers, I., & Baskin, D. (1992). Sex, race, age, and violent offending. *Violence and Victims, 7*(3), 191-201.

Spindel, D. J. (1989). *Crime and society in North Carolina, 1663-1776.* Baton Rouge: Louisiana State University Press.

Starbuck, W. H., & Milliken, F. J. (1988). *Challenger:* Fine-tuning the odds until something breaks. *Journal of Management Studies, 25*(4), 319-340.

Steffensmeier, D., & Allan, E. (1991). Gender, age, and crime. In J. F. Sheley (Ed.), *Criminology: A contemporary handbook* (pp. 67-93). Belmont, CA: Wadsworth.

Sutherland, E. (1924). *Criminology.* Philadelphia: Lippincott.

Sutherland, E. (1937). *The professional thief*. Chicago: University of Chicago Press.

Takaki, R. (1982). *Iron cages: Race and culture in 19th-century America*. New York: Alfred A. Knopf.

Taylor, S. L., & Edwards, A. (1992, February). Loving and losing Malcolm. *Essence*, 50-54, 104-110.

Thomas, W. I., & Znaniecki, F. (1958). *The Polish peasant in Europe and America*. New York: Dover.

Thorne, B. (1993). *Gender play: Girls and boys in schools*. New Brunswick, NJ: Rutgers University Press.

Thorpe, E. E. (1967). *Eros and freedom in Southern life and thought*. Durham, NC: Seeman.

Thrasher, F. M. (1927). *The gang*. Chicago: University of Chicago Press.

Tolnay, S., & Beck, E. M. (1995). *A festival of violence: An analysis of Southern lynchings, 1882-1930*. Chicago: University of Illinois Press.

Tolson, A. (1977). *The limits of masculinity* New York: Harper and Row.

Trelease, A. W. (1971). *White terror: The Klu Klux Klan conspiracy and Southern reconstruction*. New York: Harper & Row.

Turner, R. H., & Surace, S. J. (1956). Zoot suiters and Mexicans: Symbols in crowd behavior. *American Journal of Sociology, 62*(1), 14-20.

Tyler, B. M. (1989). Black jive and white repression. *Journal of Ethnic Studies, 16*(4), 31-66.

U.S. Department of Health and Human Services. (1993). *Health, United States, 1992*. Washington, DC: Government Printing Office.

Vaughan, D. (1989). Regulating risk: Implications of the *Challenger* accident. *Law and Policy, 11*(3), 330-349.

Vaughan, D. (1994, August). *Risk, workgroup culture, and the normalization of deviance: NASA and the space shuttle* Challenger. Paper presented at the annual meeting of the American Sociological Association, Los Angeles, CA.

Vaughan, D. (1996). *The* Challenger *launch decision: Risky technology, culture, and deviance at NASA*. Chicago: University of Chicago Press.

Vigil, J. D. (1988). *Barrio gangs*. Austin: University of Texas Press.

Wajcman, J. (1991). *Feminism confronts technology*. University Park: Pennsylvania State University Press.

West, C., & Fenstermaker, S. (1993). Power, inequality, and the accomplishment of gender: An ethnomethodological view. In P. England (Ed.), *Theory on gender/feminism on theory* (pp. 151-174). New York: Aldine.

West, C., & Fenstermaker, S. (1995). Doing difference. *Gender and Society, 9*(1), 8-37.

West, C., & Zimmerman, D. H. (1987). Doing gender. *Gender and Society, 1*(2), 125-151.

Wiegman, R. (1993). The anatomy of lynching. *Journal of the History of Sexuality, 3*(3), 445-467.

Williams, C. L. (1989). *Gender differences at work.* Berkeley: University of California Press.

Williams, T. M., & Kornblum, W. (1985). *Growing up poor.* Lexington, MA: Lexington Books.

Willis, P. E. (1979). Shop-floor culture, masculinity and the wage form. In J. Clarke, C. Critcher, & R. Johnson (Eds.), *Working-class culture* (pp. 185-198). London: Hutchinson.

Winant, H. (1995). Symposium. *Gender and Society, 9*(4), 503-506.

Wolfgang, M. E., & Riedel, M. (1975). Rape, racial discrimination, and the death penalty. In H. A. Bedau & C. M. Pierce (Eds.), *Capital punishment in the United States* (pp. 99-121). New York: AMS Press.

Wright, G. C. (1990). *Racial violence in Kentucky, 1865-1940: Lynchings, mob rule, and "legal lynchings."* Baton Rouge: Louisiana State University Press.

Young, I. M. (1990). *Justice and the politics of difference.* Princeton, NJ: Princeton University Press.

Zinn, H. (1980). *A people's history of the United States.* New York: Harper & Row.

Index

About the Author

James W. Messerschmidt (Ph.D., the Criminology Institute, University of Stockholm, Sweden) is Professor of Sociology and Chair of the Criminology Department at the University of Southern Maine. His research interests focus on the interrelation of gender, race, class, and crime. In addition to numerous articles and book chapters, he is author of *The Trial of Leonard Peltier* (1983), *Capitalism, Patriarchy, and Crime: Toward a Socialist Feminist Criminology* (1986), *Criminology* (2nd ed.), with Piers Beirne (1995), and *Masculinities and Crime: Critique and Reconceptualization of Theory* (1993).